COLLINS GEM

ZODIAC

The Diagram Group

HarperCollins*Publishers*

HarperCollins Publishers
P. O. Box, Glasgow G4 0NB

A Diagram Book first created by Diagram Visual Information
Limited of 195 Kentish Town Road, London NW5 8SY

First published 1993

Reprint 10 9 8 7 6 5

© Diagram Visual Information Limited 1993

ISBN 0 00 470366 9

Printed in Great Britain by
HarperCollins Manufacturing, Glasgow

Introduction

Collins Gem Zodiac Types is a clear and concise introduction to the signs of the zodiac and the behavioural characteristics they are believed to endow. Each sign and its attributes have been detailed within separate chapters. Many different aspects – from a Scorpio's personality and reactions to situations in the workplace and at home, to a Taurean's behaviour when in love – are described with the help of lists, panels and illustrations.

What is a sign of the zodiac?

Each of the 12 signs of the zodiac is a name given to a 30 degree arc of the sky, as viewed from Earth. As the Earth moves round the Sun, the Sun appears to pass from one 30 degree arc to the next, completing the journey through all 12 zodiac arcs in one year. For example, a person whose birthday is on 1 January is born when the Sun is in the zodiac sign of Capricorn. This is referred to as a person's sun sign (see 'zodiac band', p.12). Hence, a person born a month later, when the sun is passing through the next 30 degree arc, would have the next zodiac sign, Aquarius, as his sun sign.

Characteristics of the zodiac signs

The popular view is that a person will display the characteristics associated with his or her sun sign. For example, characteristics typical of Capricorn include ambition, faithfulness, weak knee joints and a long lifespan. In reality, however, many people born with the Sun in Capricorn may well have little

ambition, be unfaithful, have perfect knees or may
have died young.

What is astrology?

Astrology is the study of apparent coincidences
between certain events on Earth and the positions of
the Sun, Moon and eight planets. In traditional
terms, the Sun, Moon and planets (often loosely
called 'the stars') are said to influence events on
Earth. The modern view, first suggested by the
psychologist Carl Gustav Jung, is that events
coincide with a particular pattern of the stars. This
phenomenon is known as synchronicity.

The personal birth chart

When studying synchronicity between personality
and the stars, a complete horoscope or birth chart
must be made. This shows the positions of the Sun,
Moon and planets at the time of birth, relative to the
place of birth. The birthchart indicates many
features, only one of which is the position of the sun
at birth.

A sample birth chart

The symbols on the chart are the standard ones used
to indicate the zodiac signs, the Sun, Moon and
planets. The chart opposite is for a person born on
25 May 1931, therefore the Sun is in the zodiac sign
of Gemini. The position of the Moon at birth, the
positions of all the eight planets of the solar system
and several other important features, such as
geographical location, are all taken into account
when interpreting the chart. For example, in the
sample chart, the Moon is in Virgo, i.e. the moon
sign is Virgo. The Moon is linked with mood and

emotion, so astrologically this person's moods
would be Virgoan, rather than Geminian. A person
who had been born on the same day, in a different
year and location, however, would have a chart that
was differently oriented, although it would have
several similar features.

In very broad, general terms, this is the basis of
personal astrology.

A birth chart

See 'Astrological Symbols', p.15, for the meanings
of the symbols shown

Finding your sun sign

The approximate dates of when the Sun moves into each sign are listed below. They will be correct for most years, but incorrect for others. For example, if your birthday is 22 July, some lists will say your sun sign is Cancer, as shown below, others will say Leo.

Sign	Dates
Aries	21 March – 19 April
Taurus	20 April – 20 May
Gemini	21 May – 20 June
Cancer	21 June – 22 July
Leo	23 July – 22 August
Virgo	23 August – 22 September
Libra	23 September – 22 October
Scorpio	23 October – 21 November
Sagittarius	22 November – 21 December
Capricorn	22 December – 19 January
Aquarius	20 January – 18 Febuary
Pisces	19 February – 20 March

The cusp

The exact time when the Sun moves from one sign to the next is known as the cusp or beginning of the sign. Because the movement of the earth around the sun is not exactly regular each year, the precise date when the sun moves from one sign to the next sometimes differs.

Predictions

Future events cannot be predicted. Professional astrologers read trends by comparing a person's birth chart with the day to day movements of the Moon and the small planets (Mercury, Venus, Mars),

and the longer term movements of the larger planets
(Jupiter, Saturn, Neptune, Uranus, Pluto).

Astrology and free will

In general, astrological interpretations are
descriptions of how a person may behave rather than
what he or she might actually do. Every
characteristic has its positive and negative sides, the
interpretation of which is a matter for personal
choice; for example, one Taurean characteristic is
never to change without very good reason. This
could be interpreted either as undying loyalty or as
stubborn resistance.

How to enjoy this book

The information about each zodiac sign is a
summary of the main characteristics associated with
it. If you find that you happen to be typical of your
sun sign, it is probably because several planets are in
your sign or are linked with it in positive ways. If
you have few or none of the characteristics of your
sun sign, it could be for one or more of the
following reasons:

1 other signs are stronger in your chart;
2 your full potential has not yet emerged;
3 the characteristic has negative 'influences' in the
orientation of your chart, which you have controlled;
4 your birth date is the day of a cusp and the exact
time of birth may indicate that your sun sign is
actually in the next, or previous, sign.

Reading the sun signs is fun, and may be revealing.
If, however, you wish to investigate astrology
further, the best course of action is to have a full
chart made and interpreted by a qualified astrologer.

Contents

Glossary

air One of the four elements; associated with the intellect and thought.

astrology The study of the coincidences between planetary positions and events. While it is said that planets 'influence' events, the modern view is that coincidence is a more valid term. This view stems from the work of psychologist Carl Jung on synchronicity.

birthchart A chart showing the positions of the Sun, Moon and planets at the time of birth, relative to the place of birth.

cardinal One of the three qualities; associated with receptivity, initiative and executive action.

earth One of the four elements; associated with practical reality.

element The elements represent general characteristics that are linked with certain zodiac signs. There are four elements: fire, air, earth and water.

fire One of the four elements; associated with activity and enthusiasm.

fixed One of the three qualities; associated with stability, determination and consistency.

horoscope A birthchart calculated according to the exact time of birth.

mutable One of the three qualities; associated with adaptability, adjustment and harmonization.

opposite signs The zodiac signs opposite each other on the zodiac wheel, as follows (and vice versa):

Sign	Opposite sign
Aries	Libra
Taurus	Scorpio
Gemini	Sagittarius
Cancer	Capricorn
Leo	Aquarius
Virgo	Pisces

planets The eight major bodies, apart from Earth, which move around the Sun: Mercury, Venus, Mars, Jupiter, Saturn, Uranus, Neptune and Pluto. It is an astrological convention to also include the Sun and the Moon when speaking of the planets, making ten astrological planets in all.

quality The qualities describe behaviours associated with certain zodiac signs. There are three qualities: cardinal, fixed and mutable.

rising sign The sign of the zodiac which is on the eastern horizon at the time of birth. Also known as the Ascendent. This sign is said to indicate the general outlook, appearance, survival strategy and outer personality of people born at that time.

ruling planet Each zodiac sign is said to be especially 'influenced' by one or more of the planets, as follows:

Sign	Ruling planet
Aries	Mars
Taurus	Venus
Gemini	Mercury

Sign	Ruling planet
Cancer	Moon
Leo	Sun
Virgo	Mercury
Libra	Venus
Scorpio	Mars and Pluto
Sagittarius	Jupiter
Capricorn	Saturn
Aquarius	Saturn and Uranus
Pisces	Jupiter and Neptune

star sign Common misnomer for sun sign.

sun sign The sign of the zodiac occupied by the sun on the date of birth.

water One of the four elements; associated with sensitivity and emotion.

zodiac An imaginary band, viewed as if from the centre of the solar system, and divided into twelve segments of 30 degrees. Each segment is named after a nearby constellation of stars.

zodiac characteristics A group of characteristics associated with a sign, which have been built up from observation of events that happened when the sun was in that sign. The characteristics of people born under each sign also form a part of the astrological body of knowledge.

zodiac position The exact position of the Sun is given as between 0 and 29 degrees 59 minutes of each sign (e.g. 12 degrees 23 minutes of Capricorn, see diagram overleaf). The positions of the planets are also given in the same way. The positions at any particular time can be calculated in advance from Astronomical tables.

**Zodiac band showing
zodiac position**

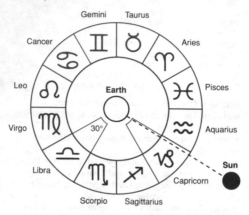

zodiac signs Twelve 30-degree segments of the
zodiac, numbered anti-clockwise according to their
positions at the spring equinox. The position of the
Sun throughout the year can be identified as 'in
Aries' (at the spring equinox and during most of
April) or 'in Libra' six months later (at the autumn
equinox and for most of October. The diagram
above shows the Sun 'in Capricorn').

zodiac wheel

Aries	1	Libra	7
Taurus	2	Scorpio	8
Gemini	3	Sagittarius	9
Cancer	4	Capricorn	10
Leo	5	Aquarius	11
Virgo	6	Pisces	12

zodiac wheel (continued)

Elements
A : Air
E : Earth
F : Fire
W : Water

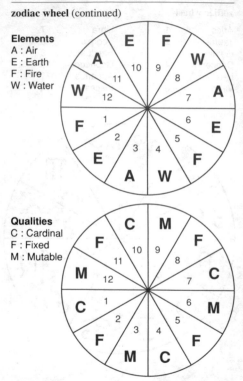

Qualities
C : Cardinal
F : Fixed
M : Mutable

Astrological symbols

The symbols used to represent the signs and their ruling planets are depicted below.

Sign	Symbol	Ruling planets	Symbols
Aries	♈	Mars	♂
Taurus	♉	Venus	♀
Gemini	♊	Mercury	☿
Cancer	♋	Moon	☽
Leo	♌	Sun	☉
Virgo	♍	Mercury	☿
Libra	♎	Venus	♀
Scorpio	♏	Mars; Pluto	♂♇
Sagittarius	♐	Jupiter	♃
Capricorn	♑	Saturn	♄
Aquarius	♒	Saturn; Uranus	♄♅
Pisces	♓	Jupiter; Neptune	♃♆

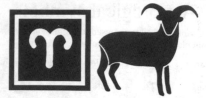

1. Aries: the Ram
21 March – 19 April

The first sign of the zodiac is concerned with
- self-assertion, initiation, new beginnings
- action, daring, challenge, adventure
- exploration, pioneering, discovering
- aggression, creativity, personal goals
- personal control of everything
- competition, winning, being first
- courage, honesty, nobility, openness

Elemental quality

Aries is the cardinal fire sign of the zodiac. It can be
likened to a fire which gives direction, such as in
a rocket, a gun or an engine. Superman and
Superwoman, who can propel themselves in any
direction, are good metaphors of Aries energy.
Fire is a process that causes change and Aries uses
energy to bring about changes. Being a cardinal
sign, Aries is the most energetic of the fire signs and
usually takes the initiative.

Spiritual goal

To learn the meaning of selfless love.

THE ARIEN PERSONALITY

These are the general personality traits found in people who are typical of Aries. An unhappy or frustrated Aries may display some of the not-so-attractive traits.

Characteristics

Positive	Negative
• Is a leader	• Must be the boss
• Is energetic	• Brashness
• Helps others to achieve their dreams	• Blind to his or her effect on others
• Accepts challenges	• Intolerance
• Believes the best of others	• Jealousy
• Takes risks for others	• Doesn't listen
• Defends the vulnerable	• Selfishness
• An Aries life is an open book	• Impulsiveness
• Will give life for the loved one	• Poor judge of character
• Continues action even if others give up	• Dislikes being told what to do

Secret Aries

Inside anyone who has strong Aries influences is a person who thinks that he or she is more interesting than others and better than those with whom they are in competition.

It is patently obvious to all that Aries is interested in winning, whoever or whatever the challenge.

A fight, a race, a bit of physical or verbal sparring or an opportunity to do things in new ways are what keep the Aries' fires burning bright. Aries is an original, and being first lights him or her up.

Aries has to be number one in every respect. The secret fear of a typical Aries is that he or she won't be liked or valued, even though a winner. However, failure is never a problem because Aries doesn't know the word . . . every outcome is seen as a part of the winning process, which is why warnings of impending disasters are usually ignored.

Ruling planet and its effect

Mars rules the zodiac sign of Aries, so anyone whose birthchart has a strong Aries influence will tend to look for challenges to overcome. In astrology, Mars is the planet of aggressive energy and creative action. Like Mars, Aries is the knight in shining armour, an inspiration to friends and a conquering hero to the underdog.

Arien lucky connections	
Colours	red, black, white
Plant	tiger lily
Gemstones	ruby, diamond
Metal	iron
Tarot card	the magician
Animals	ram and lamb

THE ARIEN LOOK

People who exhibit the physical characteristics distinctive of the sign of Aries look tall and bold. Usually lean, they have strong bodies and may even be quite athletic. They are usually concerned to project a physical image of success. They need to be winners and generally do their very best to look the part. Appearances are important to Aries.

Physical appearance

- Body: lean and strong, with large bones, thick shoulders and a rather long neck
- The face is usually long and the eyes are steady and somewhat piercing – not looking through you, but certainly looking at you, as if to challenge
- There may be a scar on the face or the body from a past fight – if so it will be 'worn' with a certain pride like a winner's trophy

THE ARIES MALE

If a man behaves in a way typical of the personality associated with the zodiac sign of Aries, he will have a tendency towards the characteristics listed below, unless there are influences in his personal birthchart that are stronger than that of his Aries sun sign.

Appearance

The typical Aries man

- has a strong body
- is extremely energetic
- has a dominating sex appeal
- walks with an air of nobility

- dresses in clothes appropriate to the current challenge

Behaviour and personality traits

The typical Aries man

- is fiercely competitive
- is honest
- appears to be self-assured
- takes initiative and expects others to follow
- is enterprising
- dreads physical disability
- has very clear goals
- will put his partner on a pedestal
- needs to win
- uses wit and brains to get what he wants

THE ARIES FEMALE

If a woman behaves in a way that is distinctive of the personality associated with the zodiac sign of Aries, she will have a tendency towards the characteristics listed below, providing there are no influences in her personal birthchart that are stronger than that of her Aries sun sign.

Appearance

The typical Aries woman

- is slim and strong
- is very active and glows with energy
- has strong, luxurious hair
- wears sophisticated colours and perfume
- dresses in clothes appropriate to the occasion

Behaviour and personality traits

The typical Aries woman

- looks you in the eye and gives a firm handshake
- is enthusiastic and optimistic
- talks back and often gets hurt because of it
- expects loyalty
- is fearless
- has interests outside the home or has a career
- expects to win through in any situation
- is direct, open and honest
- can make miracles happen

YOUNG ARIES

If a child behaves in a way that is distinctive of the personality associated with the zodiac sign of Aries, he or she will have a tendency towards the characteristics listed below.

Behaviour and personality traits

The typical Aries child

- has a strong, active body and mind
- has a temper when thwarted
- usually walks and talks early
- wants attention and to be in charge
- can be lazy until someone claims to be better
- is generous with toys
- has a vivid, practical imagination
- can achieve much in a short time
- is normally very affectionate
- has an inexhaustible curiosity
- gets over childhood fevers very quickly

Bringing up young Aries

Most Aries children are very direct about their likes
and dislikes. They are also very determined to do
things their way. Saying 'No' doesn't work, nor does
persuasion, coaxing or using other obedient children
as examples.

Young Aries children of any age respond best to a
challenge. Tell him he's probably just slow at
organizing his toys or tell her that it isn't her fault
that she can't do something very well and young
Aries goes into action, to prove he or she is better
than anyone else at anything – including doing the
things they don't like.

Young Aries' needs Adventure, opportunity to find
out, to try things, take charge, solve problems and be
a winner. Above all, Aries needs to know that he or
she is loved and valued. Big hugs and reassurance,
especially after emotional bumps, are essential,
despite the brave face they put on.

What to teach young Aries At school, Aries
children take the lead in every way and will react
against authority. So teach them when to obey by
making it a challenge.

Because Aries youngsters are so adventurous, they
ignore dangers, so parents need to be extra vigilant
about hot pans and fires. As they become old
enough, show them how to handle dangerous
situations. Don't forbid them to do things, or they
will take it as a challenge.

They need to be guided gently, with logic and praise,
not ordered about. Ask them with a smile and they
will respond with increasing confidence.

Teach Aries to handle their own money from a very early age. Explain the rights of others too, as young Aries dominates without knowing it.

They will have a few falls and show their fiery temper often, but they recover very quickly from both and come out smiling.

 ## ARIES AT HOME

If a person has the personality that is typical of those born with an Aries sun sign, home is a place to come back to after many adventures, and she or he will have a tendency towards the characteristics listed below.

Typical behaviour and abilities

When at home, an Aries man or woman

- wants to be the top dog
- makes a substantial and secure home
- doesn't like to feel tied down or restricted
- will generously give money, goods and space to those who need it
- can turn a hand to anything but doesn't enjoy those little jobs needed to run and repair a home

Aries as parent

The typical Aries parent

- won't spoil the children
- will give plenty of hugs and praise
- can create a magical fantasy world for children
- usually insists on strict discipline
- will raise children to be successful
- may try to dictate the future careers of offspring
- will fight to the death if anyone hurts the kids
- will be a devoted dad and an affectionate mum

Two Aries in the same family

Aries can be comfortably married to each other
providing they each have separate challenging
situations in their lives to confront and win. Two
Aries need to converse regularly as neither likes
being left out.

A parent and child who are both Aries will clash
many times, so the parent must recognize that young
Aries also hates being told what to do. Families with
two or more Aries can be exciting with plenty of
affection and challenge to keep them all going.

ARIES AT WORK

At work, the person who has a typical
Aries personality will exhibit the
following characteristics.

Typical behaviour and abilities

A typical Aries at work

- is loyal and enthusiastic about the company
- will work all hours and is not a clock-watcher
- will look elsewhere for an opening if bored
- is highly creative and can initiate
- has very strong willpower
- is not suited to political work

Aries as employer

A typical Aries boss (male or female)

- is idealistic and needs the faith of his or her
  employees and expects their loyalty
- believes he/she can make the future a success
- needs others but will go it alone when necessary
- wants to be recognized as the boss
- can pull a business up from near bankruptcy

- is generous with rewards for hard work
- expects everyone to drop everything to solve a crisis

Aries as employee

A typical Aries employee (male or female)

- works best when answerable only to the boss
- can promote anything
- tends to work late rather than early
- looks for opportunity to learn and progress
- intends to succeed but is careless with details
- knows he or she can do well
- will move to another job if he or she feels the challenges in the current job have run out; security is not a priority, although Aries workers usually make their way under the most difficult circumstances

Working environment

The workplace of a typical Aries man or woman

- will have people and machines to take care of the details
- may be almost anywhere that is exiting
- must be stimulating and allow freedom of movement
- will support an important-seeming image
- must be accessible at all times: day, night and weekends

Typical occupations

Aries is associated with work which inspires activity in others; for example, leaders, directors, foremen or any job that has authority. Aries must be in command or they will lose interest. Aries works best at the initiation of a project, leaving the

consolidation to other people. Typical jobs are in
recruitment and training, work in the theatre,
business enterprises, politics, sport, and the military
in any position that has power.

ARIES AND LOVE

To Aries, love is a conquest. Male Aries
love the chase and seem to have little
difficulty attracting women, while female
Aries also love the challenge of the hunt but go
about it a little more subtly. Aries of both sexes are
attractive because of their natural energy. Aries in
love will have many of the characteristics listed
below.

Behaviour when in love

The typical Aries

- is very romantic and believes in courtly love
- will insist on doing the chasing and cannot bear to
  be chased by anyone
- can be extremely possessive of the lover but
  cannot understand if the lover is possessive
- places the loved one on a pedestal
- will be jealous of any attention the loved one gives
  to others
- will defend the loved one to the death

Expectations

The typical Aries expects

- total faithfulness from the partner
- the lover to respond as if he or she is the first and
  best lover ever known
- to be loved exclusively
- never to be criticized

The end of an affair
Boredom is the blight of most Aries love affairs.
Like the knight in a crusade, it is the winning that is
the peak of excitement. Once the fair lady (or fair
gentleman) is won, there may be nothing left to
stimulate the affair further. At this point the Aries
will get itchy feet and want to be off to find new
conquests.

It isn't that love itself is merely a conquest, it is the
joy of overcoming obstacles to reach love. The
partner of an Aries must always keep a little mystery
in reserve and must always believe in every new
Aries dream. If all fails – and Aries will try and try
before leaving a relationship – then the Aries
passion cools and there remains only a lack of
interest.

A lover who hurts Aries very deeply can expect to
be totally frozen out and ignored.

ARIES AND SEX
In many ways the excitement is in the
chase not the conquest. It isn't that Aries
lovers aren't faithful – they are, so long
as the excitement of new challenges in love are
always there to stimulate them. Aries may appear to
want to dominate, but does not want a submissive
partner in sex. Routine is what brings boredom to
lovemaking for Aries. Aries woman may have
difficulties in love because she may see her partner
as a fellow contestant in the world.

ARIES AND PARTNER

The person who contemplates becoming the marriage or business partner of a typical Aries must realize that Aries will want to be in control of all the major decisions. He or she will be happy to leave the day-to-day details to a partner, but will always expect to be in overall control. Given this, the person who partners Aries can expect an exciting, creative relationship with unexpected surprises and plenty of affection.

Aries man as partner

He will want a partner of whom he can be proud, yet who will never do anything better than he can. A clever partner would be wise to be modest about personal abilities and to put effort into supporting and encouraging the sensitive Aries partner in his own dreams.

In marriage, the Aries husband will regard his wife as the queen of his domain and she must behave accordingly, never failing in her loyalty to him and keeping surprises up her sleeve to stimulate his interest.

Aries woman as partner

Like her male counterpart, the Aries partner must always come first. This makes life difficult for the typical Aries wife in a male-dominant situation. She needs a husband who will recognize and accept her powers. A man must have self-respect and tact to partner an Aries woman.

In return, both male and female Aries will bring bountiful energy, enthusiasm and loyalty to any partnership.

Opposite sign

Libra, the scales, is the complementary opposite sign to Aries. Although relationships between Aries and Libra can be difficult, Libra can show Aries how to cooperate, share and bring people together in harmony. Libra can intervene diplomatically where Aries will bound in and make demands forcibly.

ARIES AND FRIENDS
In general Aries likes a friend who is special in some particular way and who will regard Aries as his or her best friend (never the second best!).

Positive factors

Aries friends are warm and hospitable but they are
not usually interested in entertaining for its own
sake; they usually have a reason for inviting friends
around. Many Aries prefer to go out for a meal, to
find an unusual eating place. Both male and female
Aries usually get on better with male friends.

Negative factors

Because Aries are very jealous of other people's
abilities and achievements, Aries friendships often
don't last very long.

However, a person who will admire his or her Aries
friend and remain interesting him- or herself, though
not ambitious, can enjoy an enduring friendship with
Aries. Aries can become quite harsh and nasty if his
or her fragile ego is under threat.

A compatibility chart, opposite, lists those with
whom Aries is likely to have the most satisfactory
relationships.

ARIEN LEISURE INTERESTS

Most typical Aries enjoy some physical
activity that allows him or her to display
their prowess. Aries may also enjoy
board games that give them the opportunity to
demonstrate their superior mental and tactical
power.

On the whole, typical Aries pursue the following
leisure interests (continued on p. 32):

• competitive sports, e.g. football, tennis
• driving a car which has a great image
• racing by car, bicycle or on foot

Compatibility chart

In general, if people are typical of their zodiac sign, relationships between Aries and other signs (including the complementary opposite sign, Libra) are as shown below

	Harmonious	Difficult	Turbulent
Aries	●		
Taurus	●		
Gemini	●		
Cancer		●	
Leo	●		
Virgo			●
Libra		●	
Scorpio			●
Sagittarius	●		
Capricorn		●	
Aquarius	●		
Pisces	●		

- risky physical activities, such as sailing round the world single-handed or climbing a new peak
- military pastimes
- theatrical activities

Arien likes and dislikes
Likes

- being liked
- the best wines
- a unique number plate on the car
- money to use
- new clothes
- red roses
- colourful food
- personalized gifts
- presents wrapped in intriguing paper
- new books
- diamonds

Dislikes

- being ignored
- physical restriction
- being placed less than first
- feeling hungry
- anyone who performs better than them
- old things, second-hand stuff
- having to wait for anything
- lingering after food
- bland food

ARIEN HEALTH

Typical Aries are healthy and fight every illness that comes their way, staving off attacks of flu with sheer willpower. When Aries pride is hurt or life teaches a hard lesson, Aries may suffer emotionally and need great comfort. For all their apparent superiority, Aries are extremely soft-hearted and vulnerable to emotional hurts.

Types of sickness

Fevers and accidents are typical of all fire signs, especially the highly strung Aries character.

If ill, Aries will expect constant attention to his or her needs, but recovery is usually very quick.

Typical Aries may suffer from acne, epilepsy, neuralgia, headaches, migraines and baldness. Accidents due to physical activities are common, accompanied by bangs on the tough Aries head. Sinuses, eyes and ears are also vulnerable.

Aries at rest

Rarely is a typical Aries seen to rest during the day. They seem to have an inexhaustible supply of energy and a considerable willpower. However, when eventually tired, at perhaps three in the morning, the typical Aries will usually sleep well and may either sleep late or take a long time to get started again in the morning.

The typical Aries doesn't rest like most other people; both male and female Aries are too busy with some project or other to stop for long. The enthusiasm with which they do things is as good as a rest to them. When enthusiasm wanes, they still don't want to rest but are impatient to be off on a new venture.

Parts of the body linked to Aries
Traditionally, the parts of the body linked with a
strong Aries influence are as shown in the
diagram below. Only the individual birthchart will
show if one or more of these parts of the body
have inherited a strength or a vulnerability. Any
generalization would be misleading.

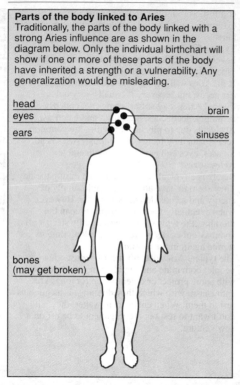

head
eyes   brain
ears   sinuses

bones
(may get broken)

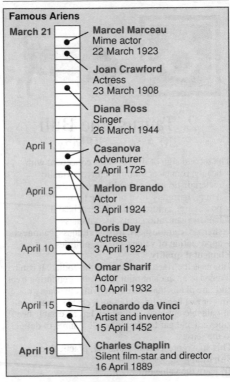

Famous Ariens

March 21

Marcel Marceau
Mime actor
22 March 1923

Joan Crawford
Actress
23 March 1908

Diana Ross
Singer
26 March 1944

April 1

Casanova
Adventurer
2 April 1725

April 5

Marlon Brando
Actor
3 April 1924

Doris Day
Actress
3 April 1924

April 10

Omar Sharif
Actor
10 April 1932

April 15

Leonardo da Vinci
Artist and inventor
15 April 1452

April 19

Charles Chaplin
Silent film-star and director
16 April 1889

2. Taurus: the Bull
20 April – 20 May

The second sign of the zodiac is concerned with
- beauty, romance, sentimentality, sensuality
- materialistic values, wealth, prosperity
- nature, harmony, love of living things
- possession, control, security, dependability
- habit, organization, tenacity, kindness
- shyness, cautiousness, trustworthiness, calmness
- appreciation of values, talents, abilities

Elemental quality

Taurus is the fixed earth sign of the zodiac. It can be likened to an ancient rainforest full of enduring trees and rare plants that is teeming with the beauty of life, or to a beautiful, old French château that is full of valuable antiques, and which has an established vineyard and garden that offer all manner of delights to the senses.

This sign represents an enduring, practical reality.

Spiritual goal

To learn the value of insight.

THE TAUREAN PERSONALITY

These are the general personality traits found in people who are typical of Taurus. An unhappy or frustrated Taurus may display some of the not-so-attractive traits.

Characteristics

Positive	Negative
• A careful and conservative outlook	• A tendency to be self-indulgent
• Dependable and offers enduring loyalty	• Can be stubborn, obstinate and get stuck in a rut
• Calm and patient	• Materialistic
• Artistic	• Slow-moving
• Thorough	• Little to say
• Attentive	• Delays action by lengthy pondering
• Values the talents of others	• Easily embarrassed
• Very loving	• Boring
• Resourceful	• Insensitivity
• Gentle and placid	
• Excellent cook	
• Good sense of time and is orderly	

Secret Taurus

Inside anyone who has strong Taurus influences is a person who takes the long-term view and proceeds slowly but surely, because Taurus is only interested in the very best of everything. Taurus's view is that the best is worth waiting for.

Taurus loves to luxuriate in sensual delights and desires secure material prosperity. The two secret fears of Taurus are of being disturbed or of being left wanting. Taurus will wait for anything, even to get angry. When Taureans do eventually have to express anger, it can be devastating and is so disturbing to themselves that it takes a while for them to recover both their composure and their self-esteem.

Ruling planet and its effect

Venus rules the zodiac sign of Taurus, so anyone whose birthchart has a strong Taurus influence will tend to have a strong set of personal values. In astrology, Venus is the planet of love, affection, values and sensuality.

Like Venus, Taureans can be very affectionate, and fond of the good life, so long as it is a peaceful, secure life. Taureans rarely detract from their personal code of what is right and proper.

Taurus, like the mythical Venus, has an idealized concept of beauty, and may, especially in early life, be very self-conscious about his or her body.

Taurean lucky connections	
Colours	pastel shades and blues
Plant	mallow
Perfume	storax
Gemstone	topaz
Metal	copper
Tarot card	hierophant (High Priest)
Animal	bull

THE TAUREAN LOOK

People who exhibit the physical characteristics distinctive of the sign of Taurus look as if they are well rooted and in touch with the earth. They may be plump or slim, but either way they will walk with a slightly ponderous gait, as if each step has been carefully considered. All typical Taureans have a presence which emanates solid reliability.

Physical appearance

- Body compact and sturdy, often with thick, muscular legs and thighs
- Face rounded with a clear, often beautiful complexion
- Neck is short and may appear rather thick if the shoulders are high and square, which is typical of those with a very strong Taurean influence
- Typical Taurean feet are large or broad
- Eyes are usually large and offer a steady gaze

THE TAURUS MALE

If a man behaves in a way typical of the personality associated with the zodiac sign of Taurus, he will have a tendency towards the characteristics listed below, unless there are influences in his personal birthchart that are stronger than that of his Taurus sun sign.

Appearance

The typical Taurus man

- has a stocky body, which is muscular if he does a lot of physical activity
- may be plump

- will bear the discomfort of an injury or disability with extreme stoicism
- has very clear skin
- is likely to have plenty of hair and can grow a substantial beard
- walks with determination

Behaviour and personality traits

The typical Taurus man

- rarely changes his point of view
- works hard to build security
- is astute and can evaluate a situation very quickly in financial terms
- is quiet and has a low-key charm
- is unpretentious
- enjoys comfort
- can be defensive and suspicious in a new or unexpected situation
- is wary of others taking advantage of him
- dresses to create an image of respectability
- uses influential connections to get what he wants

 THE TAURUS FEMALE

If a woman behaves in a way that is distinctive of the personality associated with the zodiac sign of Taurus, she will have a tendency towards the characteristics listed below, providing there are no influences in her personal birthchart that are stronger than that of her Taurus sun sign.

Appearance

The typical Taurus woman

- tends to have a rounded body

- has a beautiful complexion and hair which always looks in excellent condition
- may live by a very strict diet to attain slimness
- has an air of mystery about her because she does not flaunt her sexuality
- wears clothes which give her sensual pleasure
- has a strong body capable of hard work

Behaviour and personality traits

The typical Taurus woman

- is an introvert
- has considerable moral and emotional courage
- takes people as they come
- is very loyal to her friends and sticks by them if they are in trouble
- has practical common sense
- is deeply sensual
- prefers the real to the artificial, e.g. real flowers, real silk and genuine, high-quality antiques

YOUNG TAURUS

If a child behaves in a way that is distinctive of the personality associated with the zodiac sign of Taurus, he or she will have a tendency towards the characteristics listed below.

Behaviour and personality traits

The typical Taurus child

- is usually a quiet baby with rare outbursts
- is stubborn and wants his or her own way
- has a strong little body and can often be found clenching his or her fists when opposed
- is usually calm, pleasant and a little shy

- is cuddly and affectionate
- dislikes being the centre of attention
- responds to common sense and affection
- usually works slowly but steadily at school

Bringing up young Taurus

Never try to force a young Taurus to do something because the Taurean child will turn stubborn and will always hold his or her ground longer than anyone else, except perhaps a Taurean parent. Harsh commands will never discipline the young Taurus, but a loving hug will melt all the resistance out of that obstinate little bull.

Both girls and boys are usually competent little people and open to practical, common-sense explanations. Both can charm adults, especially of the opposite sex.

Young Taurus's needs Physical affection given freely and without smothering is essential to the healthy growth of any Taurean child. Young Taurus also needs harmonious surroundings. Colours and sound will affect these children quite deeply. Harmonious blues, shades of pink and rose and soft sounds will be calming and reassuring.

What to teach young Taurus Most children who are typically Taurean will have soft, melodious voices so they should be introduced to singing or other forms of music from an early age. Usually these children will prefer melodious music to noisy modern pop; nor will nursery rhymes satisfy them for long. Let them hear a wide selection of classical music which they can absorb into their·souls. Drawing, colouring and other artistic activities –

such as collage with materials lovely to the touch –
will please and stimulate young Taurus.

In general, Taurean children will take a clear,
practical and orderly approach to school work. They
need to be given time to learn, but things once learnt
are not forgotten. Taureans should be encouraged to
communicate, through words, pictures and music as
they tend to hide their true feelings behind silent
obstinacy.

TAURUS AT HOME

If a person has the personality that is
typical of those born with a Taurus sun
sign, home is a place to feel absolutely
secure and comfortable. The person who has strong
Taurean influences will have a tendency towards the
characteristics listed below.

Typical behaviour and abilities

When at home, a Taurus man or woman

- hates anything to be moved around
- enjoys comfort and luxury
- has well-tried habits and likes a well-ordered
  household
- prefers to own his or her home
- makes his or her home a castle and usually fills it
  with furniture that will increase in value

Taurus as parent

The typical Taurus parent

- is affectionate
- has seemingly endless patience
- can be rather dominant and possessive
- may find it hard to relax and play with the children

- will support, encourage, nurture and protect the children with unswerving faith in their own abilities as a parent
- will teach self-respect
- will save for the future
- expects high standards

Two Taureans in the same family

Taureans can get on well together providing they have similar personal values. If they disagree about fundamental issues, their obstinacy could lead to a permanent impasse as neither will give an inch. On the other hand, their mutual placidity and response to physical affection should overcome any serious disagreements.

 TAURUS AT WORK

At work, the person who has a typical Taurean personality will exhibit the following characteristics.

Typical behaviour and abilities

A typical Taurus at work

- will work steadily towards achieving what he/she values
- cannot bear interference
- has great respect for institutions
- requires work that gives respectability

Taurus as employer

A typical Taurus boss (male or female)

- patiently tests out the employees
- doggedly sticks to his stated principles
- will give everyone more than a fair chance but sack anyone who breaks his or her trust

- is often a self-made person and will make money
- does not make hasty judgements
- wants things done his or her way
- is kind and patient but expects total loyalty
- likes plain facts and hates flattery

Taurus as employee

A typical Taurus employee (male or female)

- needs a regular salary
- is an excellent person to handle money
- is honest and dependable
- is practical, sensible and down-to-earth
- enjoys sensible routines
- displays foresight
- is rarely thrown off-balance
- can handle emergencies

Working environment

The workplace of a typical Taurus man or woman

- must be calm and well ordered
- any noise or colour scheme must be low key, if it is an office
- should be at a fixed location – rural or parkland settings suit Taurus well

Typical occupations

Taurus is associated with banking, farming, floristry, interior design, architecture, food, engineering, building, general medical practice, executive secretarial positions, stable occupations in established institutions and any occupation that involves the shrewd acquisition of land, investments or goods.

TAURUS AND LOVE

To Taurus, love is a physical, sensual romance which can be expected to last for ever. Taureans are attracted by physical beauty and are very sensitive to perfume, colour, light and sound. Taurus in love will have many of the characteristics listed below.

Behaviour when in love

The typical Taurus
- is devoted and steadfast
- settles quickly into a stable affair
- loves glamour
- is extremely vulnerable to people who accept his or her affection but only want a flirtation
- will never forgive a betrayal
- the male is generally the strong silent type
- the female is usually an earth mother/Venus

Expectations

The typical Taurus expects
- his woman to be very feminine
- her man to be all male
- a promise to be kept and never broken
- a wholesome, natural approach to physical love
- to be pampered
- to wait for a commitment to be made

The end of an affair

It takes a long time for a Taurean to decide to leave a relationship. Taurus finds it extremely difficult to be convinced he or she was wrong about a person. However, once the Taurean mind is made up, there is never any turning back. He or she will walk away for ever.

Being a good judge of character is not one of
Taurus's strengths, so some will assume all is well,
even when a lover is being deceitful. When a deceit
is revealed, Taurus will be very hurt but will still
hang on in hope.

Some Taurus men can be rather macho, so when a
relationship is ending, the macho Taurus can lose his
normally gentle approach, becoming harsh and
domineering. This usually indicates the hurt to his
ego, which at heart is very trusting and naive.

The lover who walks out on a Taurean will leave
behind a bewildered, disbelieving person, who may
suffer one vague illness after another as the hurt and
rage slowly come to the surface.

TAURUS AND SEX

When a typical Taurus makes love it is
the most physical and natural pleasure in
the whole world. Sex is never a power
game for a Taurean, it is something very natural to
be enjoyed. Taureans, especially females, are
sometimes embarrassed about their bodies if they
feel they are being criticized. On the whole, Taurus
regards nudity as natural and wholesome.

TAURUS AND PARTNER

The person who contemplates becoming
the marriage or business partner of a
typical Taurus must realize that Taurus
will expect absolute loyalty through thick and thin
and will probably want to establish a routine way of
doing things his or her way.

Given this, the person who partners Taurus can expect honest devotion, a long-term relationship and a partner who can keep his or her head in any emergency.

Taurus man as partner

He will want a partner who enjoys his way of doing things. The partner should be prepared to take the responsibility for good public relations while Taurus works quietly away ensuring that money and power come their way.

The Taurean husband wants a marriage partner whom he can possess, body, soul and dowry. He needs a woman who enjoys physical love, since to Taureans there is no division between love, sex and marriage.

Taurus woman as partner

She will want a partner who is attentive and appreciative. Common sense is essential in any partner of a Taurean. She, like her male counterpart, will look for a business partner who will bring prestige to the business.

The Taurean wife wants to be given gifts and treated with gentleness. She does not want to be patronized, but she does want her man to remember her birthday and other anniversaries.

She needs a husband who will let her organize at least a part of his life and who will never, never give her cause for jealousy.

Opposite sign

Scorpio is the complementary opposite sign to Taurus. Although relations between Taurus and Scorpio can be difficult because they are both stubborn signs, Scorpio can show Taurus how to gain insight into the needs and motives of other people, and thus also into his or her own life. In this way, Taurus can use his or her natural sensitivity to help in the service of others.

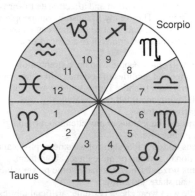

TAURUS AND FRIENDS

In general Taurus likes a friend who is reliable, unchanging and not given to sudden excitement or changes of plans.

Positive factors

Taureans are very warm and affectionate towards their friends. They enjoy friendship with people who have good taste and with whom they can enjoy a quiet conversation or a visit to a concert or a football match.

They will enjoy people who have strength of character and qualities of endurance like their own. Towards such friends, Taurus will always be gentle, kind, loving and totally trustworthy.

Negative factors

Taurus can be jealous of any attention a friend gives to someone else.

Taurus does not like signs of weakness, physical or emotional, and can be quite direct about them.

Taurus prizes friends who have some power which they can share and enjoy.

People who wear cheap perfume, artificial fabrics and have houses that are built to deceive the eye, e.g. not real stone but stone-faced, are unlikely to attract the friendship of a typical Taurean.

A compatibility chart, opposite, lists those with whom Taurus is likely to have the most satisfactory relationships.

Compatibility chart
In general, if people are typical of their zodiac sign, relationships between Taurus and other signs (including the complementary opposite sign, Scorpio) are as shown below

	Harmonious	Difficult	Turbulent
Taurus	●		
Gemini	●		
Cancer	●		
Leo		●	
Virgo	●		
Libra			●
Scorpio		●	
Sagittarius			●
Capricorn	●		
Aquarius		●	
Pisces	●		
Aries	●		

♈ ♉ ♊ ♋ ♌ ♍ ♎ ♏ ♐ ♑ ♒ ♓

TAUREAN LEISURE INTERESTS

On the whole, typical Taureans pursue the following leisure interests:

- collecting things of value
- singing or listening to music
- gardening
- painting
- the quieter sports
- activities that give Taurus a chance to enjoy physical pleasure, such as horse-riding

Taurean likes and dislikes

Likes

- soft, sensual textures
- sensual pleasures
- a good bank balance
- certainty and well-tried routines
- gifts of value,
- attractively wrapped
- savouring the moments of pleasure at the table
- doing the same thing over and over

Dislikes

- being disturbed
- change
- lending things
- being told to hurry up
- sleeping in strange beds

TAUREAN HEALTH

Typical Taureans are robust people. They may suffer from being a little overweight, but on the whole Taurus is healthy, provided nothing comes along to disturb the status quo. A Taurus who has an unsatisfactory sex life will be rather like a bull with a sore head . . . fractious and prone to grunting and grumbling. The greatest danger for Taurus comes from their ability to hold back anger and to stubbornly hold on to a redundant point of view. That can lead to melancholy and medical depression.

Types of sickness

Infections of the throat are said to be linked with Taurus, including laryngitis, swollen glands and croup. Constipation may also bother a Taurean. When ill or if involved (untypically) in a serious accident, Taurus can withstand any amount of discomfort and pain. The Taurean ability to stubbornly refuse to allow anything to get the better of him or her is a great advantage during times of sickness. Similarly, a Taurean will stand by family and any friend who has a misfortune.

Taurus at rest

Extending the metaphor of the fixed earth sign, Taurus at rest is totally relaxed and lazy. In fact, Taurus can rest with feet up in front of the television or listening to music for days and days.
Taureans usually sleep well and wake up slowly. Once they are on the go again, they can keep going for long periods without feeling tired.

Parts of the body linked to Taurus
Traditionally, the parts of the body linked with a
strong Taurus influence are as shown in the
diagram below. Only the individual birthchart will
show if one or more of these parts of the body
have inherited a strength or a vulnerability. Any
generalization would be misleading.

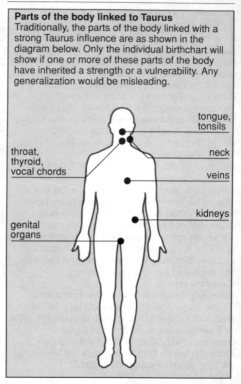

tongue,
tonsils

neck

throat,
thyroid,
vocal chords

veins

kidneys

genital
organs

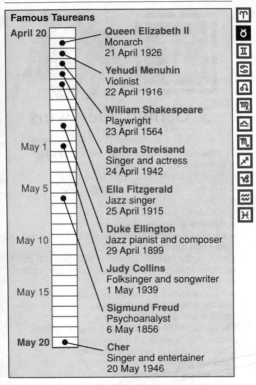

Famous Taureans

April 20

Queen Elizabeth II
Monarch
21 April 1926

Yehudi Menuhin
Violinist
22 April 1916

William Shakespeare
Playwright
23 April 1564

May 1

Barbra Streisand
Singer and actress
24 April 1942

May 5

Ella Fitzgerald
Jazz singer
25 April 1915

Duke Ellington
Jazz pianist and composer
29 April 1899

May 10

Judy Collins
Folksinger and songwriter
1 May 1939

May 15

Sigmund Freud
Psychoanalyst
6 May 1856

May 20

Cher
Singer and entertainer
20 May 1946

3. Gemini: the Twins
21 May – 20 June

The third sign of the zodiac is concerned with
- communication, articulation, speech
- dexterity, nimbleness, light-footedness
- wit, instinct, persuasion, change, variety
- movement, curiosity, exploration, short journeys
- education, learning, collecting facts
- attention to details, adaptability
- intellect, intuition, youth, freedom

Elemental quality

Gemini is the mutable air sign of the zodiac. It can be likened to the wind in that it is constantly on the move in all its variety.

Air is a metaphor for the invisible thoughts and ideas that motivate Gemini, such as the intellect, the intuition and the natural instincts.

The quality known as mutable means adaptable, changeable, agreeable. Gemini constantly adjusts ideas in an attempt to create harmony.

Spiritual goal

To learn how to cooperate.

THE GEMINIAN PERSONALITY
These are the general personality traits found in people who are typical of Gemini. An unhappy or frustrated Gemini may display some of the not-so-attractive traits.

Characteristics	
Positive	Negative
• Inquisitive	• Restless
• Entertaining and charming	• Quickly bored
• Versatile	• Impractical
• Liberal, broad minded	• Impatient and irritable
• Youthful	• Capricious and fickle
• Quick	• Gossipy
• Stimulating	• Nervous
• Inventive	• Manipulative
• Never prejudiced	• Non-committal
	• Dual personality

Secret Gemini
Inside anyone who has strong Gemini influences is a person who secretly longs to find his or her true soul-mate, the mysterious twin who will make the Gemini feel complete. The more self-aware Geminis will realize in maturity that the wholeness they seek is to be found within, by gathering together their many parts, especially the earthly twin with the spiritual twin.

Few people listening to a confident Gemini talk with that quicksilver, puck-like charm would ever imagine that the inner Gemini is often feeling desperately alone and lost.

Communication is a life-line to Gemini. Contact through words, ideas, gossip or philosophy makes Gemini a happy, inspiring and devoted person.

Ruling planet and its effect

Mercury rules the zodiac sign of Gemini, so anyone whose birthchart has a strong Gemini influence will tend to be on the go, moving to and fro with many messages like the fleet-footed Mercury of mythology, who was the eloquent messenger of the gods.

Mercury wore a winged helmet and carried the caduceus, a stick round which were entwined twin snakes. The snakes represent the libido and the healing powers of the instinctual mind.

In astrology, Mercury is the planet of thought and communication, and governs all mental and nervous processes. Mercury is the hermaphrodite of the zodiac, taking the neutral position of mediator between the masculine and feminine viewpoints. Mercury is the planet of duality, the translator, who speaks in two languages that link body and soul.

Geminian lucky connections	
Colour	orange
Plants	orchid and hybrids
Perfume	lavender
Gemstones	tourmaline and garnet
Metal	quicksilver
Tarot card	the lovers
Animal	magpie

THE GEMINIAN LOOK

People who exhibit the physical characteristics distinctive of the sign of Gemini look tall and upright.

The youthful look is typical of Gemini. People who always look younger than their actual age, at any stage of life, will have a strong Gemini influence somewhere in their birthchart.

Most typical Geminians are light on their feet, regardless of their body size.

Physical appearance

● Body: usually slim. However, if the zodiac neighbours of Gemini, Taurus and Cancer, are present in the birthchart they may affect the body-build, because the signs of both Taurus and Cancer can lead to plumpness. A strong Taurus influence, particularly, can lead to a weight problem.

● Generally tall

● Strong and active

● Long arms and legs

● Fleshy hands

THE GEMINI MALE

If a man behaves in a way typical of the personality associated with the zodiac sign of Gemini, he will have a tendency towards the characteristics listed below, unless there are influences in his personal birthchart that are stronger than that of his Gemini sun sign.

Appearance

The typical Gemini man

● is taller than average

- has a pale, rough complexion that will become
  weather-beaten easily
- is very agile
- has a high forehead and receding hairline
- has quick, darting eyes

Behaviour and personality traits

The typical Gemini man

- is eager and always on the move
- is friendly and persuasive
- can sell almost anything to almost anyone
- has a great deal of nervous energy
- can talk himself out of difficulties
- can do two things at once
- likes people
- is adroit, diplomatic and socially able
- may change his occupation frequently
- is intelligent and witty

 THE GEMINI FEMALE

If a woman behaves in a way that is
distinctive of the personality associated
with the zodiac sign of Gemini, she will
have a tendency towards the characteristics listed
below, providing there are no influences in her
personal birthchart that are stronger than that of her
Gemini sun sign.

Appearance

The typical Gemini woman

- is tall and slender, unless there is a strong Taurus
  influence causing plumpness
- has very fine eyes
- has long arms and legs

- has exquisitely expressive hands
- moves quickly

Behaviour and personality traits

The typical Gemini woman
- is a lively conversationalist
- has many interests
- is a composite of many personalities
- is a great friend, taking an interest in any new subject
- will want to have a career
- seeks true romance but finds it hard to settle down
- is a deep thinker and often very intuitive
- will never turn down a cry for help
- is optimistic
- notices every detail
- can be charming and very persuasive

YOUNG GEMINI

If a child behaves in a way that is distinctive of the personality associated with the zodiac sign of Gemini, he or she will have a tendency towards the characteristics listed below.

Behaviour and personality traits

The typical Gemini child
- can seem to be in two places at once
- loves chattering
- will become irritable if cooped up
- needs lots of space to explore
- is friendly
- is bright and alert

- can be quite precocious
- usually learns to read very quickly
- likes to use his or her hands and fingers
- may be ambidextrous
- can often mimic others

Bringing up young Gemini

Most Geminis have an insatiable inquisitiveness about everything. They like to explore, follow whatever catches their interest and get their fingers into everything, quite literally.

Gemini children tend to live in a world where imagination and reality are so mixed together that it is hard for them to learn where one begins and the other ends.

These children will want to be friends with both sexes. As they grow up, they will have a variety of boyfriends or girlfriends. When they actually become emotionally involved with someone (or something) they will often pretend they are not at all interested, because emotional involvement leaves them totally confused.

Children of both sexes will be keenly interested in a wide variety of sports.

Young Gemini's needs The Gemini child needs the freedom to explore, investigate and learn. Frequent opportunities to change direction, and follow several lines of interest at once, are essential.

They need to be understood more than anything. The love that Gemini children need is the attention of those who accept them for what they are and go along with them in their dreams.

Confinement or boredom are the worst horrors to a little Gemini.

What to teach young Gemini Young Gemini should be taught how to distinguish between illusion and reality. Encouraging him or her to always tell the truth will help this to happen. Gemini children are naturally honest and will only avoid telling the truth as a defence against feeling misunderstood. These children will enjoy learning to communicate, to read and to speak several languages. They can easily become bilingual if spoken to in different languages from an early age.

Teaching a Gemini to slow down a little can be difficult but will help the young Gemini to be more selective in later years, as Geminis tend to throw out old ideas and pursuits indiscriminately.

GEMINI AT HOME

If a person has the personality that is typical of those born with a Gemini sun sign, home is a place to return to after yet another period of travel.

The Gemini at home will have a tendency towards the characteristics listed below.

Typical behaviour and abilities

When at home, a Gemini man or woman

- likes space to move about in
- will enjoy using gadgets and all the latest technology, especially information technology
- considers a telephone absolutely essential
- will have some form of transport standing by so he or she can take off on the spur of the moment

- will have a bright, cheerful home, surrounded by the evidence of many interests
- enjoys company
- has a deep need for tenderness and emotional warmth for which he or she finds it very hard to ask

Gemini as parent

The typical Gemini parent

- can get on a child's wavelength very easily
- will enjoy playing with and teaching his or her children
- may find it hard to show his or her real emotions
- uses rational arguments to explain things

Two Geminis in the same family

Unless one or both have planets in the earthy or fixed signs, two Geminis in one family means there will be at least four personalities flitting around. Geminis can get on well, provided both have enough space. They will happily chat together, absorbing and discussing all the new facts they can find. However, if two Geminis get into an emotional argument, sparks fly because Geminis can be very confused by and feel threatened by strong emotions, especially their own.

GEMINI AT WORK

At work, the person who has a typical Gemini personality will exhibit the following characteristics.

Typical behaviour and abilities

A typical Gemini at work

- gets things done

- works better with people around
- can deal with emergencies quickly
- will try anything once
- needs variety

Gemini as employer

A typical Gemini boss (male or female)

- is not dogmatic
- delegates astutely and concentrates on schemes to increase profits and cut costs
- makes changes to improve communication and productivity
- is impatient with mundane administration
- will inspect, notice and question every aspect of every department
- will classify his or her workers' talents
- enjoys building goodwill and large order books by meeting clients in restaurants, on the golf course, or anywhere out on the road in places near or far

Gemini as employee

A typical Gemini employee (male or female)

- can charm his or her way through an interview
- is good at thinking, new ideas and details
- chats, makes jokes and gets things done
- will get bored and fail to carry through an idea if too much red tape holds up a project
- enjoys fast action and quick returns

Working environment

The workplace of a typical Gemini man or woman

- (if it has to be in a fixed place) must be spacious and stimulating

Typical occupations

Geminis are good in any kind of work that involves public relations, selling or getting information and ideas across to others such as lecturing, journalism and work in any of the media. Their quick minds, combined with dextrous abilities, make some into surgeons, scientific researchers, artists or musicians. Because they love words and ideas, they may become politicians or actors.

GEMINI AND LOVE

To Gemini, love is a romantic ideal which can only be achieved with the soul-mate. Consequently, many Geminis may flirt and have frequent affairs, looking for that perfect romantic love. The characteristics of Gemini in love are listed below.

Behaviour when in love

The typical Gemini

- is overwhelmed by confusing emotions
- may appear cool and distant
- will think things through rather than act spontaneously
- needs a rational understanding of love
- tends to repress very strong emotions
- is acutely sensitive and open to hurt
- can become emotionally dependent
- feels very deeply but finds it very hard to express love

Expectations

The typical Gemini expects

- to be understood

- the partner to be an emotional telepath
- sympathy and tenderness
- personal freedom for self and partner
- to enjoy flirting
- faithfulness of partner

The end of an affair

An affair will end when a Gemini gets bored or
when a partner begins to make too many emotional
demands or restrict the Gemini's personal freedom.
The end may seem like a sudden decision, but it
never is; the decision to leave a lover will have been
made only after much mental unhappiness.

Once the decision has been made, Geminis have no
difficulty in communicating that an affair is at an
end, they just cool off, freeze the partner out or
vanish.

If the partner ends the relationship, Gemini will be
deeply hurt and feel insecure and at a loss. The more
outward Geminis may hide these feelings behind a
sudden outburst of scathing anger, while the quieter
ones will probably try to look cool. Either way,
Gemini will put on a show of confidence and
continue searching for perfect love.

GEMINI AND SEX

When a typical Gemini makes love it is
often a drive to express all their pent-up
emotions at once. Geminis seek variety
in love, enjoy surprises and plenty of light-hearted
romance. Geminis are often not interested in sex for
its own sake, they want more from a partner, even in
a short relationship, such as companionship and

warmth. Love and sex belong together in the eyes of
a Gemini.

The most erogenous zone of a typical Gemini is the
mind. Talk excites, while silence turns off the
Gemini.

GEMINI AND PARTNER

The person who contemplates becoming
the marriage or business partner of a
typical Gemini must realize that Gemini
has probably already had more than one partner and
will not stay long with a person who either clings or
dominates.

Given this, the person who partners a Gemini can
expect the talents of at least six people wrapped up
in the one Gemini.

Gemini man as partner

He will want a partner who will never attempt to
dominate him, nor bore him with endless personal
problems.

He will be drawn either to someone who will help
him on his way up the professional or social scale,
or a person who will stimulate him with bright ideas.
Because he loves to travel, he will be delighted in a
partner who will travel with him – or accept his
absences without question.

Gemini woman as partner

She will be attracted to a person who can give her
emotional security where she can relax and enjoy
expressing her many talents, and her 'multi-
personality'. Often the partnership will be short-
lived because the restless Gemini nature always

wants to be on the move. Many partners fail to understand the need of the mercurial butterfly to have a partner who will fly with her, helping her to find the peace she truly desires.

Opposite sign

Sagittarius is the complementary opposite sign to Gemini. From Sagittarius, Gemini can learn to take a broader view of things and to give some structure to the mass of information they collect – and so eventually find the truth.

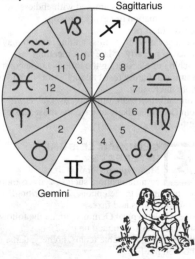

Sagittarius

Gemini

GEMINI AND FRIENDS

In general, Gemini likes a friend who is curious about the world and enjoys lively, intelligent conversation.

Positive factors

Geminis generally enjoy people who respond to, or suggest, spontaneous activities.

They will run to your help when you are in need.

A Gemini friend is full of life, often a Peter Pan, and always eager to be off on a new adventure.

They will keep friends amused with endless stories, bits of information or network gossip.

Negative factors

Gemini never wants to miss a thing, and so may be inclined to be early or late for a meeting.

Stretching or elaborating the truth is not uncommon; Geminis can hardly resist adding extra spice to make it more interesting.

A compatibility chart, opposite, lists those with whom Gemini is likely to have the most satisfactory relationships.

GEMINIAN LEISURE INTERESTS

Most typical Geminis like communication, such as conversation, radio, television, the telephone, letter writing, sending postcards and faxes.

On the whole, typical Geminis pursue the following leisure interests (continued on p. 72):

• 'light' sports, e.g. table tennis, archery, darts, snooker, pool

Compatibility chart

In general, if people are typical of their zodiac sign, relationships between Gemini and other signs (including the complementary opposite sign, Sagittarius) are as shown below

	Harmonious	Difficult	Turbulent
Gemini	●		
Cancer	●		
Leo	●		
Virgo		●	
Libra	●		
Scorpio			●
Sagittarius		●	
Capricorn			●
Aquarius	●		
Pisces		●	
Aries	●		
Taurus	●		

- travel, short or long journeys
- newspapers, magazines, quizzes, crosswords
- public-speaking, variety shows, dancing
- discovering and exploring something new
- learning and using languages
- using hands and fingers for crafts etc.

Geminian likes and dislikes

Likes

- being free to move about
- the excitement of travel
- chatting
- telephones, gadgets, instant food
- acting as devil's advocate
- doing several things at once
- knowledge, information
- acting quickly on decisions
- variety, novelty, change
- company; being among people
- pseudonyms
- getting to the bottom of things

Dislikes

- listening to endless complaints
- regimentation
- not knowing what's going on
- wasting time
- being kept waiting
- making irrevocable commitments
- being defeated
- fixed ideas
- having to concentrate on only one thing for a long time

GEMINIAN HEALTH

Typical Geminis are healthy so long as they have plenty of room to breathe and space to explore. They are liable to nervous exhaustion if they don't find a personally satisfying way to relax. Geminis are not often heard to complain. On the rare times when sickness strikes them down, they may get irritated when well-intentioned people ask how they are. They much prefer to be amused by some interesting news, than have to relate the details of their infirmity.

Types of sickness

Coughs, colds, bronchitis, speech problems and other chest/lung complaints are most typical of Geminian ill-health. Whenever physical misfortune strikes, the person who behaves in the way typical of Gemini is likely to hide the most serious side of things and make even less of the least serious aspect. Geminis usually hate being confined to bed and are restless until they finally exhaust themselves. At this point they become still, silent and heavy, like the closeness that occurs before the thunderstorm breaks and all is well again.

Gemini at rest

There is no such animal as a Gemini at rest. Even when seemingly relaxed by a winter's fire after playing in the snow with the children all afternoon, the Gemini mind will be at work, inventing a new gadget to make, thinking up a new idea, working over a problem or rehearsing a conversation to be held with a colleague.

Parts of the body linked to Gemini
Traditionally, the parts of the body linked with a strong Gemini influence are as shown in the diagram below. Only the individual birthchart will show if one or more of these parts of the body have inherited a strength or a vulnerability. Any generalization would be misleading.

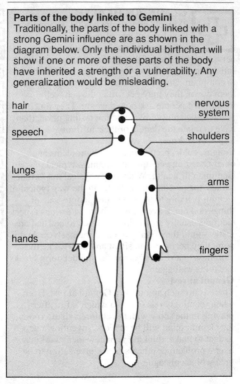

hair

nervous system

speech

shoulders

lungs

arms

hands

fingers

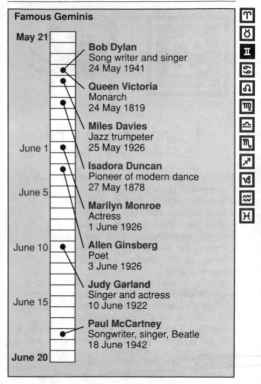

Famous Geminis

May 21

Bob Dylan
Song writer and singer
24 May 1941

Queen Victoria
Monarch
24 May 1819

Miles Davies
Jazz trumpeter
25 May 1926

June 1

Isadora Duncan
Pioneer of modern dance
27 May 1878

June 5

Marilyn Monroe
Actress
1 June 1926

June 10

Allen Ginsberg
Poet
3 June 1926

Judy Garland
Singer and actress
10 June 1922

June 15

Paul McCartney
Songwriter, singer, Beatle
18 June 1942

June 20

4. Cancer: the Crab
21 June – 22 July

The fourth sign of the zodiac is concerned with
- receptivity, sensitivity, defence
- home, protection, comfort, domesticity
- food, nurture, mothering instincts
- nostalgia, sentiment, roots, antiques
- money, business, response to public need
- dreams, the psychic, telepathy etc.
- family, history, memory, patriotism

Elemental quality

Cancer is the cardinal water sign of the zodiac. It
can be likened to a safe harbour where boats can
take shelter from the dangers on the sea of life.
Water finds its own level – it settles. The
metaphorical harbour is the way Cancer provides a
safe and organized place for human activity, setting
each ship in its allotted place.

Spiritual goal

To learn how to take a balanced view of things.

THE CANCERIAN PERSONALITY

These are the general personality traits found in people who are typical of this sign. An unhappy or frustrated Cancerian may display some of the not-so-attractive traits.

Characteristics

Positive	Negative
• Tenacious	• Possessive
• Shrewd and intuitive	• Too easily hurt
• Kind	• Moody
• Compassionate	• Crabby
• Domesticated	• Matriarchal
• Good memory	• Holds on to insults
• Helpful	• Selfish
• Caring	• Manipulative
• Sensitive to need	• Introspective
• Protective	• Overpowering

Secret Cancer

Inside anyone who has strong Cancerian influences is a person who was very shy when young and who still tends to use a hard outer shell in defence against what are perceived as hurts from other people. The most vulnerable part of the Cancerian personality is an inner fear of nameless dangers that often reduce a wonderful dream to a pessimistic worry. The fear is of becoming lost in the dark of outer space. This indefinable fear of insecurity is often what drives the typical Cancerian personality to invest much time and effort in activities which will enhance a feeling of security and self-preservation.

Ruling planet and its effect

The moon rules the zodiac sign of Cancer, so anyone whose birthchart has a strong Cancerian influence will absorb and accurately reflect every emotion that is experienced.

In astrology, the moon's cycle of waxing and waning is a metaphor for the cycle of changing moods of the Cancerian personality, who can experience periods of wondrous elation and of crabby depression.

The moon is also associated with oddities and, when in the mood, Cancerian humour can be quite crazy – almost lunatic. Cancerian humour provides some of the best comedy in the world of entertainment, because it is always based on an accurate observation of human nature.

Cancerian lucky connections	
Colours	yellow-orange and indigo
Plants	lotus, moonwort and almond
Perfume	onycha
Gemstones	pearl, amber and moonstone
Metal	silver
Tarot card	the chariot
Animals	crab, turtle and sphinx

THE CANCERIAN LOOK

People who exhibit the physical characteristics distinctive of the sign of Cancer are of three facial types.

Whichever type they are, they have very expressive faces. Every mood, emotion and fleeting response shows in the changing features of the Cancerian face.

Physical appearance

- Body: usually top heavy; can be slim, but often on the plump side
- Face 1: rather crab-like with a large head, high cheekbones and prominent brows. Eyes small and far apart
- Face 2: rather moon-like and baby-faced, round with soft skin, a wide mouth and a charming grin. Eyes are usually round
- Face 3: a combination of the two above, but distinctive, with especially strong cheekbones

THE CANCER MALE

If a man behaves in a way typical of the personality associated with the zodiac sign of Cancer, he will have a tendency towards the characteristics listed below, unless there are influences in his personal birthchart that are stronger than that of his Cancer sun sign.

Appearance

The typical Cancer man
- has a fairly bony structure
- may have remarkable teeth, perhaps prominent, irregular or in some way unusual

- if crab-faced he will have a prominent lower jaw
- may have broad shoulders
- even if slim may appear broad or plump
- may be plump or tend to put on weight very easily

Behaviour and personality traits

The typical Cancerian man

- is extremely sensitive
- wears clothes with a conservative cut
- does not like to be conspicuous
- has some favourite old casual clothes which he always wears; he would be very cranky if anyone threw out his precious old jumper
- does not push himself into the limelight
- enjoys the limelight if it turns on him for a while
- dislikes discussing his personal life
- loves security, money, food and children
- uses round-about tactics to get what he wants
- has an uncanny business sense
- is usually very attached to his mother

THE CANCER FEMALE

If a woman behaves in a way that is distinctive of the personality associated with the zodiac sign of Cancer, she will have a tendency towards the characteristics listed below, providing there are no influences in her personal birthchart that are stronger than that of her Cancer sun sign.

Appearance

The typical Cancer woman

- has a face that is typically round and soft but may be a crab-type as described above

- may be flat-chested or have a large bust
- has hips that are often slimmer than her bust
- puts on weight easily in middle age
- has a strong bone structure
- has very expressive eyes
- has long arms and legs compared with body
- has large and long or small and chubby hands and feet

Behaviour and personality traits

The typical Cancer woman

- is introspective and emotional
- uses her intuition more often than logic
- will use all her maternal instincts to care for and protect friends and family
- wants material security and comfort
- never does anything impulsively
- is shy but very sexual
- easily takes umbrage at minor insults
- is patient, subtle and often unconsciously manipulative

YOUNG CANCER

If a child behaves in a way that is distinctive of the personality associated with the zodiac sign of Cancer, he or she will have a tendency towards the characteristics listed below.

Behaviour and personality traits

The typical Cancer child

- changes mood frequently
- loves delicious food and drinks but almost always dribbles even when past babyhood

- is fascinated by colours and pictures
- will remember every experience right into adulthood
- longs to be hugged, loved, and encouraged
- withdraws inwardly from any kind of rejection
- can play alone for hours
- often invents invisible playmates
- may cry a lot and use tears to get what he or she wants
- when older, Cancerian children seek any kind of job to earn money and save it

Bringing up young Cancer
Most Cancerians are delightful, fascinating children whose faces show every changing mood. They love to use their imaginations and are easy to manage and discipline when young, providing they are given a lot of warmth, approval and attention.

Parents should laugh and cry with a Cancerian infant and give constant reassurance when he or she is fearful, which is likely to be often.

Cancerian children are usually docile and good mannered, but prefer to be the leader rather than the follower.

Young Cancer's needs Cancerian children are very sensitive to emotional hurts and rejections and must have parental support at these times. If they feel rejected and unloved they will grow up to be reclusive, withdrawing permanently inside their shell in self-protection.

What to teach young Cancer A Cancerian child needs to feel free to express his or her emotions in poetry, painting, story-making, music-making, acting or any other form of creative activity. Thus, young Cancer should be taught the basic techniques and given the space and materials to enable him or her to express things adequately.

The parents of a Cancerian child must find a middle way between too much firmness and too much spoiling. Teaching the young Cancerian to use his or her natural instincts to care for others is a very good way of achieving this.

A clear and quick punishment will do no harm when it is necessary, providing it is balanced with much physical affection at other times.

When Cancerian children use their vivid imaginations to exaggerate the truth, they should be taught to distinguish between reality and imagination. They need plenty of outlet for their imagination.

CANCER AT HOME

If a person has the personality that is typical of those born with a Cancer sun sign, home is a place which must offer complete security and he or she will have a tendency towards the characteristics listed below.

Typical behaviour and abilities

At home, a Cancerian man or woman
- is capable of most kinds of D.I.Y.
- can cook and will keep a well-stocked larder
- feels safe and secure and so can relax
- will tend the garden
- may have collections of antiques
- spoils all visitors

- will hoard anything seen as potentially valuable

Cancer as parent

The typical Cancerian parent

- may worry too much about their offspring
- will protect and support the children
- may be over-possessive
- will enjoy looking after and playing with the babies
- will do anything to help and encourage the children's creative development
- remembers every birthday and anniversary

Two Cancerians in the same family

If the mutual need for security and reassurance can be satisfied, two Cancerians can get on well. Their greatest conflicts will arise when they disagree about intuitive matters. Together they can work very well at a money-making activity. The Cancerian sensitivity may result in some highly emotional moments, but so long as each person has a creative outlet, all will be well.

The Cancerian sense of humour should be encouraged and will relax any stressful moments that arise from Cancerian selfishness.

CANCER AT WORK

At work, the person who has a typical Cancerian personality will exhibit the following characteristics.

Typical behaviour and abilities

A typical Cancerian at work

- is there to make money
- takes work seriously and works hard

- will take responsibility
- responds to affectionate appreciation
- works steadily and is reliable

Cancer as employer

A typical Cancerian boss (male or female)
- expects his or her people to be neatly dressed
- takes work seriously and does not like frivolity
- has one aim: to make money
- drives a hard bargain but is fair
- rarely forgets anything
- generously rewards hard work

Cancer as employee

A typical Cancerian employee (male or female)
- will work hard for money because a good bank balance makes him or her feel secure
- will accept discipline calmly
- expects the rate of pay to increase steadily in response to increased output and responsibility
- enjoys taking responsibility

Working environment

The workplace of a typical Cancerian man or woman
- must be comfortable and secure
- will have family photos displayed
- will be organized for hard work
- should be furnished with the best-quality tools
- a location near water would be an added bonus

Typical occupations

Occupations that attract typical Cancerians are the food industry, such as baking, confectionery, catering, nutrition, hotel or domestic work; animal breeding, horticulture, gardening; anything connected with boats, water, ponds, rivers, fountains, baths, fishing; any kind of trading; counselling, psychotherapy, social services, nursing, obstetrics; political work connected with any of these.

CANCER AND LOVE

For a Cancerian, love thrives when there is a combination of constant affection with a healthy bank balance and substantial assets.

A Cancerian in love will have many of the characteristics listed below.

Behaviour when in love

The typical Cancerian

- will rarely make the first move
- fears he or she will be rejected
- will retreat, deeply hurt, at the first sign of ridicule or criticism
- will respond to honest warmth and affection
- can become tenaciously attached to the loved one
- is a romantic at heart
- will put the loved one first in all things

Expectations

The typical Cancerian expects

- to be loved for ever
- to have his or her cooking appreciated
- to work hard for money and security
- the family to come first in all things
- to be needed as a tower of strength and refuge
- unshakable loyalty and devotion

The end of an affair

The confusion between emotional hunger and love can lead to relationship problems. Cancerians often feel they are not loved enough, and so make draining demands on any partner who seems to have become disinterested. The Cancerian will cling more tightly as a relationship deteriorates, making separation very difficult.

If the partner has been unfaithful, the Cancerian will become very jealous and may react aggressively because the hurt is so great.

On the other hand, a Cancerian who feels unloved may secretly wander off to find someone else to satisfy their strong emotional needs. Even so, they will resist divorce, no matter how unpleasant the marriage becomes as a consequence.

CANCER AND SEX

Love and sex are synonymous to the typical Cancer, as are love and marriage. The Cancerian does not want a complicated sex life. The place where a Cancerian makes love must be secure and help him or her to relax.

Cancerians tend to dramatize love and can become very strongly attached to someone who never intended to make a commitment and therefore cannot reciprocate their feelings.

CANCER AND PARTNER

The person who contemplates becoming the marriage or business partner of a typical Cancerian must realize that Cancer will want to be the dominant partner and will expect total devotion.

Given this, the person who partners Cancer can expect consideration, prosperity and a strong sense of belonging to family or company. The contented Cancerian will never let the partner down.

Cancerian man as partner

He will want a partner who will mother him and take care of all the domestic details, making sure he has a comfortable nest to return to after a day's work.

In marriage or business, he will want others around him. If the marriage proves to be childless, adoption or fostering are likely.

A business is itself seen as a family. He will not usually enjoy working freelance.

Cancerian woman as partner

She will seek a partner as soon as she leaves the parental home – someone who will luxuriate in her protective caring.

She will devote herself completely to the partner, even taking subtle control of him or her.

In business, she will be an excellent manager.

A Cancerian woman will want a family, and if denied the joy of children will acquire a household full of animals instead.

The Cancerian wife is never a sleeping-partner when it comes to earning money. She will take a job outside the home to enhance the family's financial security.

Opposite sign

Capricorn is the complementary opposite sign to Cancer, and forms the paternal complement to Cancerian maternalism. From Capricorn the Cancerian can learn how to distinguish reality from imagination, thus getting things into a proper perspective and consequently making better judgements.

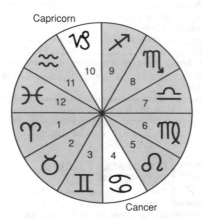

Capricorn

Cancer

CANCER AND FRIENDS

In general, Cancer likes friends who will support his or her emotional and financial needs when necessary – and Cancer will reciprocate.

Positive factors

Friends are, in many ways, regarded as family possessions themselves and are treated as such, with loving care, protective hospitality, sensitive consideration and great tenderness.

Although some friends may come and go, friends from younger days are the most precious.

Negative factors

When he or she is hurt by a friend, the Cancerian anger may last for a long time and the friend may be abandoned. However, if the friend is an old friend, then the emotional attachment will finally lead to reconciliation.

Cancerians do tend to set their own standards by the progress his or her friends are making.

A compatibility chart, opposite, lists those with whom a Cancerian is likely to have the most satisfactory relationships.

CANCERIAN LEISURE INTERESTS

Not fond of heavy exercise, Cancerians may join clubs or causes that allow an outlet for making complaints and putting their maternal instincts to good use.

Consumer affairs rouse their interest and they will follow popular interests in the arts.

Compatibility chart
In general, if people are typical of their zodiac sign, relationships between Cancer and other signs (including the complementary opposite sign, Capricorn) are as shown below

	Harmonious	Difficult	Turbulent
Cancer	●		
Leo	●		
Virgo	●		
Libra		●	
Scorpio	●		
Sagittarius			●
Capricorn		●	
Aquarius			●
Pisces	●		
Aries		●	
Taurus	●		
Gemini	●		

On the whole, typical Cancerians pursue the
following leisure interests:

- boating, sailing, swimming
- water sports that are played in teams
- fishing and gardening
- keeping and breeding animals
- building collections
- keeping in contact with family members

Cancerian likes and dislikes

Likes

- anyone who loves his or her mother
- sentimental and family keepsakes
- gourmet food
- shopping trips
- history, especially family genealogy
- any demonstration of affection such as flowers
- a birthday card on the right date
- the company of other people
- a calm working atmosphere
- physical contact

Dislikes

- any tiny criticism of the home
- having to handle a crisis
- pressure to take part in conversation
- anyone who refuses their cooking
- people who forget names and dates (Cancerians have excellent memories themselves)

CANCERIAN HEALTH

Typical Cancerians are calm, docile people able to withstand sickness so long as they have material security, plenty of affection and are needed by several people. Their greatest problems can arise from worries caused by a lack of these things.

Types of sickness

Some Cancerians are complainers when they feel not enough affectionate attention is coming their way, yet when an illness slowly creeps up on them they are remarkably tough and complain less and less. A melancholy or full depression may then be evident.

Typical illnesses often arise from the upper digestive tract, especially the stomach. Indigestion, catarrh, coughs, anaemia and lowered vitality are common. Cancerians may also suffer from eating disorders.

Cancer at rest

Extending the metaphor of Cancer as the cardinal water sign, it follows that emotion in action is the key to understanding how Cancerians relax.

Although they do enjoy lounging around, preferably on or near water, they are at their most relaxed when their busy emotional sensors are satisfied by being surrounded by the warmth of a contented family atmosphere.

When on holiday, Cancerians most enjoy a home from home, which may mean a luxurious caravan. They can also relax in the peace of a comfortably furnished period house, and generally prefer old buildings to modern styles.

Parts of the body linked to Cancer
Traditionally, the parts of the body linked with a
strong Cancer influence are as shown in the
diagram below. Only the individual birthchart will
show if one or more of these parts of the body
have inherited a strength or a vulnerability. Any
generalization would be misleading.

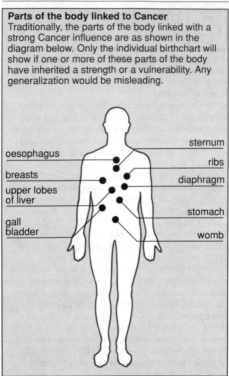

oesophagus

breasts

upper lobes
of liver

gall
bladder

sternum

ribs

diaphragm

stomach

womb

Famous Cancerians

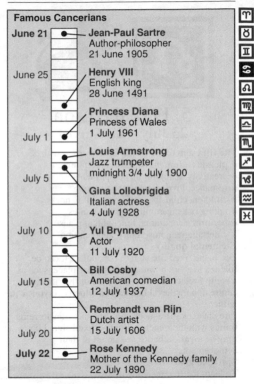

June 21 — **Jean-Paul Sartre**
Author-philosopher
21 June 1905

June 25 — **Henry VIII**
English king
28 June 1491

— **Princess Diana**
Princess of Wales
July 1 — 1 July 1961

— **Louis Armstrong**
Jazz trumpeter
July 5 — midnight 3/4 July 1900

— **Gina Lollobrigida**
Italian actress
4 July 1928

July 10 — **Yul Brynner**
Actor
11 July 1920

— **Bill Cosby**
American comedian
July 15 — 12 July 1937

— **Rembrandt van Rijn**
Dutch artist
July 20 — 15 July 1606

July 22 — **Rose Kennedy**
Mother of the Kennedy family
22 July 1890

5. Leo: the Lion
23 July – 22 August

The fifth sign of the zodiac is concerned with

- pleasures, fun, playfulness, entertainment
- creativity, recognition, compliments
- romance, love affairs, sex, offspring
- children, child-like activities, childishness
- taking risks, gambling, sports, games
- performance, drama, limelight, applause
- entertainment, hospitality, appreciation

Elemental quality

Leo is the fixed fire sign of the zodiac. It can be likened to a fire burning in its proper place, such as a camp fire, a home fire in a grate or the fire at the centre of a medieval hall around which everyone can gather.

Fire changes substances and Leos like transforming things with their energy. Being a fixed sign, Leos may be loyal, stubborn and proud of their achievements.

Spiritual goal

To learn the true meaning of love.

THE LEONINE PERSONALITY

These are the general personality traits found in people who are typical of this sun sign. Unhappy or frustrated Leos may display some of the not-so-attractive traits.

Characteristics

Positive	Negative
• Honesty and loyalty	• Stubborness or wilfulness
• A sunny disposition	• Contempt or arrogance
• A sense of dignity	• Sulkiness
• Pride in the home	• Smugness or boastfulness
• Attractive liveliness	• Indifference or an uncaring attitude
• Friendliness and kindness	• A tendency to take undue credit
• Generosity and hospitality	• A tendency to cut others down to size
• Acceptance of people at face value	• A tendency to keep up appearances
• A mature sense of responsibility	• Cold-heartedness when hurt
• Courageousness to the point of self-sacrifice	

Secret Leo

Inside anyone who has strong Leo influences is a person who wants to be on top. Potential competitors should remember this. Leo is not interested in winning, but in being king or queen of a particular castle.

Privately, the typical Leo craves love more than

anyone would ever guess. Love, adoration,
appreciation, recognition: these are what keep Leo's
generous, fun-loving nature burning brightly. While
typical Leos may appear to be confident, especially
when they take centre-stage in the limelight, they
have secret doubts about their true worth and may
seriously undervalue themselves.

Ruling planet and its effect

The Sun rules the zodiac sign of Leo, so anyone
whose birthchart has a strong Leo influence, may
expect things in life to orbit around them.

In astrology, the sun is the life-giver and the source
of creativity. Like the Sun, Leos can be a source of
life-enhancing warmth, joy and pleasure to friends
and family.

Leonine lucky connections	
Colours	yellow and orange
Plants	sunflower and laurel
Perfume	olibanum
Gemstones	catseye and chrysolite
Metal	gold
Tarot card	fortitude
Animal	lion

THE LEONINE LOOK

People who exhibit the physical characteristics distinctive of the sign of Leo look majestic. They may seem tall if (typically) they are proud of their appearance. They are either very particular about their looks or apparently somewhat careless. Either way their appearance catches the attention of others – a usual Leo trait.

Physical appearance

- Body: slim and graceful in movement
- Hair: long or short, bushy and curly or straight – a feature of pride which they emphasize by stroking, running their fingers through their locks or playing with a curl
- Baldness: a Leo will either wear a fine hairpiece or make the bald head a feature!
- Face: oval with large eyes
- Voice: strong

THE LEO MALE

If a man behaves in a way typical of the personality associated with the zodiac sign of Leo, he will have a tendency towards the characteristics listed below, unless there are influences in his personal birthchart that are stronger than that of his Leo sun sign.

Appearance

The typical Leo man

- has a well-proportioned body
- is slim and athletic if he takes care of himself
- if disabled will fight to regain prowess in some aspect of sport

- has sex appeal and may be a playboy when young
- walks tall with a noble bearing
- dresses to impress

Behaviour and personality traits

The typical Leo man
- likes to show off
- is trusting
- appears to be in control of himself
- gives and expects loyalty
- likes everything he does to be exciting
- is generous with affection and money
- likes an elegant environment
- is popular
- needs to be adored
- uses charm to get what he wants

 THE LEO FEMALE

If a woman behaves in a way that is distinctive of the personality associated with the zodiac sign of Leo, she will have a tendency towards the characteristics listed below, providing there are no influences in her personal birthchart that are stronger than that of her Leo sun sign.

Appearance

The typical Leo woman
- is slim and elegant
- if disabled will use the disability to advantage, making it attractive
- has sex appeal
- appears to possess an inner sense of royalty
- is well-dressed

- looks attractive even in adverse circumstances
- exudes dignity and class

Behaviour and personality traits

The typical Leo woman

- likes to show off in subtle ways
- is trusting and loyal
- is never docile or adoring in affairs of the heart but gives respect, warmth and real emotional commitment
- likes everything she does to be exciting
- is generous with affection and hospitality
- likes an elegant environment
- is a social leader
- needs to be admired
- uses courtesy to get what she wants

YOUNG LEO

If a child behaves in a way that is distinctive of the personality associated with the zodiac sign of Leo, he or she will have a tendency towards the characteristics listed below.

Behaviour and personality traits

The typical Leo child

- is sunny and friendly
- has a bottomless well of energy
- is more often on the move than still
- loves games and physical play
- when tired often falls fast asleep for a while
- loves to be the centre of attention
- adventurous and sometimes reckless
- likes to be waited on

- dislikes menial tasks
- loves parties
- is generous with whatever is seen as his or hers

Bringing up young Leo

Most Leos enjoy the limelight at school and often take the lead. As they grow up they will be attracted to the opposite sex and fall in and out of love. Their emotions will be turbulent and often dramatic.

To be able to grow and experiment both sexes need freedom, which they will use well if they have become used to a discipline that is tempered with love.

Leo girls may go through a truly tomboy phase as they are naturally happiest when doing something physical.

Young Leo's needs Young Leo needs plenty of love and honest compliments. Lies, even flattering ones, are very hurtful to the trusting Leo child. He or she also needs a good balance of affection and discipline: plenty of hugs and praise for their achievements.

What to teach young Leo Young Leo should be taught from early on that too much boasting is undignified. This explanation will probably work because even in the messiest situations, Leo likes to keep his or her dignity.

The friendly Leo nature endears Leo children to everyone, including strangers. Leo children should be watched over very carefully until they are old enough to understand that not everyone is as warm-hearted as they are.

Young Leo needs to be trained to take a share in the

jobs around the home. If not, doting parents may find a little tyrant on their hands. If the jobs are given special titles, little Leos will enjoy doing even menial tasks.

He or she needs to be taught about the importance of regular study and given an understanding of the rights of others.

He or she should be taught to handle money, including the need to save it, as they are likely use it generously.

LEO AT HOME

If a person has the personality that is typical of those born with a Leo sun sign, home is their natural territory and he or she will have a tendency towards the characteristics listed below.

Typical behaviour and abilities

At home, a Leo man or woman

- rules the roost
- creates an elegant, comfortable home
- offers superb hospitality
- expects others to respect his or her territory
- is able to fix most practical things
- enjoys entertaining
- shows courage and strength in emergencies

Leo as parent

The typical Leo parent

- is conscientious about bringing up children
- wants to be proud of offspring
- may put too much pressure to succeed on children
- expects to be loved and appreciated by offspring

- is capable of giving great warmth
- knows how to play with children
- is generous with pocket money
- insists on honesty
- makes every effort to teach children many things

Two Leos in the same family

Leos can be happily married to each other once they realize they both have similar needs for love and adoration. Two Leos in the same family, whether parents or children, can get on well together if they each have a castle of their own on which they can stand and be admired. Each needs to be a leader in their own field.

If one feels he is receiving less praise than the other, there could be some very dramatic quarrels.

Otherwise, a home with Leos in it will be a happy, exciting and relaxing place.

LEO AT WORK

At work, the person who has a typical Leo personality will exhibit the following characteristics.

Typical behaviour and abilities

A typical Leo at work

- gives a good first impression at interviews
- is able to act a part or exaggerate when necessary
- must be in charge of something
- can work very hard
- finds it difficult to apologize

Leo as employer

A typical Leo boss (male or female)

- has huge self-confidence

- can get everyone working hard for him or her
- loses confidence if his authority is undermined
- is thoughtful towards workers and their families
- is generous with praise and compliments
- enjoys showing people how to do things
- tends to take the credit for everyone's success
- cannot tolerate failure
- can charm people into working devotedly

Leo as employee

A typical Leo employee (male or female)
- needs to have his or her superiority recognized
- works hard
- is very loyal
- can keep customers happy
- makes a good showperson
- responds to genuine praise of his or her efforts

Working environment

The workplace of a typical Leo man or woman
- is convenient and comfortable
- has an air of luxury
- usually has pictures on the wall
- often has status symbols displayed
- is a place that inspires admiration

Typical occupations

Leo is often associated with leadership, promotion and sales, any job which has a special title, acting, directing, teaching, politics, public relations, management, the law or a self-employed trade. Leo often shows his or her inner strengths when under great pressure or when a crisis occurs.

LEO AND LOVE

To Leo, love is a dramatic ideal. Male Leos seem to have no trouble attracting women, while female Leos attract many men with their natural beauty and liveliness. The typical Leo in love will have many of the characteristics listed below.

Behaviour when in love

The typical Leo

- is romantic and proud of it
- becomes more regal and noble
- is very generous to the person who is loved
- is attentive and loyal to the loved one
- is radiant with happiness
- is caring, protective and supportive
- will make great sacrifices for love
- will fight to the death for the loved one

Expectations

The typical Leo expects

- to be adored by the loved one
- to be the envy of others
- to be treated like royalty
- his or her love to be seen as very special
- total commitment from the loved one
- the partner to be dependent in some way

The end of an affair

If Leo's passions cool, the partner is still needed, but more as a friend than a lover, which may cause problems and lead to parting or divorce if the partner does not like this arrangement. When a Leo wants to end an affair of the heart, pride may make it very difficult for the Leo to say straight out that things

are at an end. Consequently, some Leos deal with
this problem by withdrawing from contact or even
by behaving badly towards the partner. If the partner
does not confront the Leo and continues to cling, he
or she can become quite psychologically cruel,
treating the discarded partner with disdain.

The partner who is unfaithful to Leo, or who walks
out on a serious love affair, will leave behind a very
wounded person. It will take Leo months to recover
from such a deep hurt and may make him or her
very wary of risking serious love again.

LEO AND SEX

When a typical Leo makes love it is
regarded as a many splendored thing. In
fact, Leos can often forget about their
partners as they wander through their personal,
playful world of lovemaking. Leos are unrestrained
lovers and can make the partner feel very special.
Any idea of failure is alien to both male and female
Leos. If sexual problems arise, a typical Leo is
mortified and often will not seek the help that is
needed. The sexual partner is also required to be a
friend. In fact, the Leo wants love, sex and
friendship from his or her spouse or lover.

LEO AND PARTNER

The person who contemplates becoming the marriage or business partner of a typical Leo must realize that Leo will believe him- or herself to be superior in some way or other. Given this, the person who partners a Leo can expect warmth, loyalty, support, generosity and undying devotion. Only lazy, foolish Leos look for a partner who will worship them.

Leo man as partner

He will want a partner who enhances his own image and who enjoys being in the spotlight as much as he does. The partner must be good-looking but should not outshine Leo himself. Leo man wants a marriage partner who will place him at the head of the table and believe in his dreams. She will be a woman of good manners who will never do anything to tarnish her own, and therefore his, reputation and she will be a devoted mother to their children.

Leo woman as partner

The typical Leo woman looks for a partner who will install her as queen of the whole neighbourhood. He must provide her with a house she can make into a welcoming place, where she can entertain with enthusiasm and be Lady Bountiful.

With the right partner, a lady Leo will rise in social status due to her boundless strength and persistence. Consequently, her light will shine on her partner too. Leo woman will take the responsibility of motherhood in her stride and will expect her partner to be as devoted to the children as she is.

Opposite sign

Aquarius, the water-carrier, is the complementary
opposite sign to Leo. There may be tough relations
between them, but Aquarius can show Leo how to
share without needing appreciation, and give the
centre stage to others. In this way Leos can learn to
stand alone and value themselves.

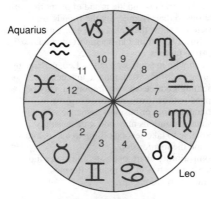

LEO AND FRIENDS

In general, Leos like their friends to be successful, but not so successful as to completely outshine and detract from Leo!

Positive factors

Leos are friendly, warm and often playful. They enjoy their friends and are proud of them; they are generous to their friends, but the friends are expected to show their gratitude, either in kind or by performance, putting Leo's support to good use.

Negative factors

A friend who in some way fails a Leo, perhaps by seeming to criticize or failing to appreciate something Leo sees as very important, may be dropped without explanation.

A friend, partner or business associate who has personal aspirations may find it increasingly impossible to take second billing to a Leo, and so may end the relationship.

A compatibility chart, opposite, illustrates those with whom Leo is likely to have the most satisfactory relationships.

LEONINE LEISURE INTERESTS

Most typical Leos like to follow a fitness routine. Done sensibly, this will strengthen any weak points. As Leos always want to be outstanding in anything they do, they should beware of overdoing exercise – it may make them vulnerable to stress reactions.

Compatibility chart
In general, if people are typical of their zodiac sign, relationships between Leo and other signs (including the complementary opposite sign, Aquarius) are as shown below

	Harmonious	Difficult	Turbulent
Leo	●		
Virgo	●		
Libra	●		
Scorpio		●	
Sagittarius	●		
Capricorn			●
Aquarius		●	
Pisces			●
Aries	●		
Taurus		●	
Gemini	●		
Cancer	●		

On the whole, typical Leos pursue the following leisure interests:

- any sport that offers skill with grace
- tennis, diving, running, dancing
- car driving, rallying, cycling
- theatre and dramatic activities
- family party games
- eating out

Leonine likes and dislikes

Likes

- activity
- anything that promises pleasure
- being creative, e.g. gourmet cooking
- receiving birthday cards
- beautifully wrapped, personalized gifts
- silks, satins, gold
- receiving thanks
- an appreciative audience
- sincere compliments
- children and pets
- unusual food and new recipes
- exotic drinks
- luxury furnishings
- top-quality, fashionable clothes

Dislikes

- physical hurt
- sedentary activities
- being ignored
- being backstage
- lies and deceit
- being laughed at
- being told something they don't know
- one-upmanship

LEONINE HEALTH

Typical Leos are happy, healthy, energetic people so long as they are loved. Only when seriously deprived of affection or appreciation will a Leo tend to look haggard and be heard moaning about life.

Types of sickness

High fevers, sudden illnesses and accidents are typical of Leonine ill-health. Whatever physical misfortune strikes, the person who behaves in a way typical of Leo will enjoy only a brief period of being spoilt in the sick bed before he or she is up again and on the go. To be incapacitated for long is a sign of weakness to a Leo. This desire to get up too soon after an illness may mean that a health problem recurs.

Leo at rest

Extending the metaphor of Leo as the fixed fire sign, it follows that the fire in the grate will sometimes burn brightly and be a centre of warmth and delight to everyone who gathers around it. However, fires do go out and have to be re-lit. So it is with typical Leonine energy. The Leo will sometimes need to rest, relax and have catnaps. This should not be mistaken for incipient sickness or laziness. Once revitalized, the typical Leo will be on the go again for hours.

Parts of the body linked to Leo
Traditionally, the parts of the body linked with a strong Leo influence are as shown in the diagram below. Only the individual birthchart will show if one or more of these parts of the body have inherited a strength or a vulnerability. Any generalization would be misleading.

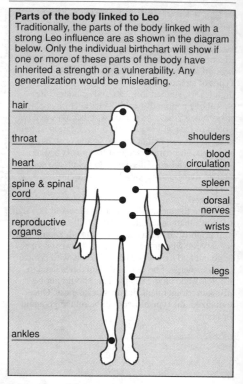

hair

throat

heart

spine & spinal cord

reproductive organs

shoulders

blood circulation

spleen

dorsal nerves

wrists

legs

ankles

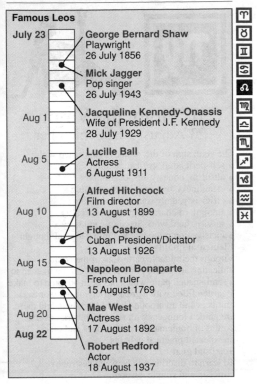

Famous Leos

July 23

George Bernard Shaw
Playwright
26 July 1856

Mick Jagger
Pop singer
26 July 1943

Jacqueline Kennedy-Onassis
Wife of President J.F. Kennedy
28 July 1929

Aug 1

Lucille Ball
Actress
6 August 1911

Aug 5

Alfred Hitchcock
Film director
13 August 1899

Aug 10

Fidel Castro
Cuban President/Dictator
13 August 1926

Aug 15

Napoleon Bonaparte
French ruler
15 August 1769

Mae West
Actress
17 August 1892

Aug 20

Aug 22

Robert Redford
Actor
18 August 1937

6. Virgo: the Virgin
23 August – 22 September

The sixth sign of the zodiac is concerned with
- self-perfection, critical faculties
- altruism, honesty, responsibility
- cleanliness, hygiene, health, healing
- efficiency, daily routines, reliability
- strength of character, veiled sensuality
- service, hard work, passivity, modesty
- incisive communication, shrewd logical thought

Elemental quality

Virgo is the mutable earth sign of the zodiac, indicating adaptable practicality. It can be likened to a semi-shaded patio which has been adapted to make a garden filled with a great variety of pot plants, climbers and an arbour. Half hidden, here and there, are garden loungers with rich patchwork covers, bottles of homemade organic wines and other unexpected practical delights.

Spiritual goal

To learn to discriminate between destructive criticism and simple wisdom.

THE VIRGOAN PERSONALITY

These are the general personality traits found in people who are typical of Virgo. An unhappy or frustrated Virgo may display some of the not-so-attractive traits.

Characteristics

Positive	Negative
● Gentleness with the helpless	● Scathing criticism of the lazy
● Sympathetic	● Cranky and irritable
● Humane and helpful	● Dogmatic
● Organized	● Untidy
● Knowledgeable about good health	● Tendency to be a hypochondriac
● Witty and charming	● Nervous and worried
● Physically sensual	● Prudish
● Painstaking	● Eccentric
● Emotionally warm	● Undemonstrative
● Dedicated	● Overdemanding

Secret Virgo

Inside anyone who has strong Virgo influences is a person who worries too much about every personal imperfection and is never satisfied with his or her own standards. Virgo may appear to know it all and be a compulsive worker; both these behaviours hide a deep fear that he or she cannot be good enough for, say, the job or the partner.

Virgos crave the opportunity to serve others and take charge of the many apparently mundane matters that, collectively, are the bedrock of success.

One of the least suspected aspects of a Virgo personality is a strong, almost volcanic sexuality that can lie hidden and dormant for years until the right partner comes along.

Ruling planet and its effect

Mercury rules the zodiac sign of Virgo, so anyone whose birthchart has a strong Virgo influence will have a good and quick mind.

In astrology, Mercury is the planet of the mind and communication. Being more concerned with practicalities than ideas (Gemini, the ideas sign, is also ruled by Mercury), Virgo is usually interested in acquiring information and in communicating by writing.

The other traditional ruler of Virgo is the mythological Vulcan, the lame god of thunder, who had a confident and brilliant mind.

Virgoan lucky connections	
Colours	yellow-green, brown, cream
Plants	narcissus, vervain, herbs
Perfume	narcissus
Gemstones	peridot, opal, agate
Metal	mercury
Tarot card	the hermit
Animals	bat, porcupine, mink

THE VIRGOAN LOOK

People who exhibit the physical characteristics distinctive of the sign of Virgo look neat and fastidious and have a pleasant, often quietly beautiful face. Many Virgos look like loners and are not usually noisy people.

Physical appearance

- High forehead
- Cranium may seem too big in comparison with the face
- Eyelids are often veiled
- Nose is straight
- Jaw is broad

THE VIRGO MALE

If a man behaves in a way typical of the personality associated with the zodiac sign of Virgo, he will have a tendency towards the characteristics listed below, unless there are influences in his personal birthchart that are stronger than that of his Virgo sun sign.

Appearance

The typical Virgo man

- has a straight, wedge-shaped nose
- has an extremely large forehead
- has a high hairline
- is upright and has a straight body
- may be quite tall
- often has one foot turned in more than the other

Behaviour and personality traits

The typical Virgo man

- is practical and unsentimental

- instinctively has a love of work
- will be devoted to serving those less fortunate than himself
- may relax by working a little less hard than usual
- takes responsibilities seriously
- is subtle and rarely obvious about his intentions
- notices and remembers details

THE VIRGO FEMALE

If a woman behaves in a way that is distinctive of the personality associated with the zodiac sign of Virgo, she will have a tendency towards the characteristics listed below, providing there are no influences in her personal birthchart that are stronger than that of her Virgo sun sign.

Appearance

The typical Virgo woman
- has a pointed chin and a face in repose
- the eyes are often soft and very beautiful
- the hair may be long or short but is normally impeccably groomed
- the mouth and lips are well formed
- is typically clean and very neatly dressed

Behaviour and personality traits

The typical Virgo woman
- can analyse situations in detail
- is devoted to her work, usually serving others in some way
- is basically shy
- has incredible strength of purpose
- will pursue happiness wherever it leads

- is pure-minded but not naive
- thinks of herself as more orderly and efficient than other people
- has a delightful, straightforward personality
- does not express her feelings easily
- can be soothing one moment and critical the next

YOUNG VIRGO

If a child behaves in a way that is distinctive of the personality associated with the zodiac sign of Virgo, he or she will have a tendency towards the characteristics listed below.

Behaviour and personality traits

The typical Virgo child

- is quick, alert and an excellent mimic, and so can learn many things in a short time
- gets upset if he or she forgets something that has been learned by heart
- rarely questions authority but frequently questions facts
- is honest and reliable
- is usually shy among strangers
- loves to do jobs around the home imitating an adult
- is sometimes a fussy eater
- is usually tidy, with occasional bouts of disorganization
- gets very upset if teased
- is often an early talker and reader

Bringing up young Virgo

Young Virgos will try very hard to please, so long as
he or she knows what is expected.

As they grow up they will often find close
relationships with the opposite sex very difficult.
Virgos take a lot of convincing that they are
attractive people. Lots of genuine praise and
encouragement early in life will help to smooth the
path to true love in teenage and early adulthood.
Parents should never interfere when their young
Virgo begins to notice the opposite sex. Even the
slightest hint of criticism or teasing may cause
Virgos to withdraw and choose the single life.

Young Virgo's needs Young Virgo must have
physical affection, in the form of hugs and sincere
compliments every day in order to build the self-
confidence that every typical Virgo child lacks.

What to teach young Virgo Myths, fairy stories,
make-believe, daydreams and how to use
imagination should all be taught to young Virgos so
they have plenty of magical moments to remember
in their adult years when they often feel lonely.

On the whole, young Virgos aim for good results at
school, are helpful round the house and are usually
tidy about their own things, almost to a fault. An
untidy Virgo will have some other strong influence
in the astrological birthchart.

Virgos can be exacting about time, orderliness and
about his or her food. They also have a tendency to
be critical about everyone else in the family,
especially when asked an opinion. They therefore
need to be taught to accept the little foibles of other

people and not to get upset when someone else leaves the top off the toothpaste.

VIRGO AT HOME

If a person has the personality that is typical of those born with a Virgo sun sign, home is a place where they will thrive, and he or she will have a tendency towards the characteristics listed below.

Typical behaviour and abilities

When at home, a Virgo man or woman

- enjoys being head of the household
- is domesticated in most areas such as cooking, managing the household finances, general maintenance, health, hygiene and gardening
- will always be doing or making something
- is usually at his or her most relaxed
- pursues several hobbies at or from home

Virgo as parent

The typical Virgo parent

- encourages children to ask questions
- supports practical activities during free time
- worries about the children's health
- is helpful, especially about detailed work
- can adapt to almost any practical demand
- may find it hard to express affection warmly
- gets upset by children's dirt and untidiness
- will explain demands he or she makes
- will do anything to help their children

Two Virgos in the same family

Married to each other, or as members of the same family, Virgos can get on very well. But difficulties will arise if they become too critical of each other and undermine each other's confidence. On the whole, however, Virgos are made of sterner stuff and can adapt their practical arrangements to accommodate any serious differences. Normally their mutual need for cleanliness and tidiness works very well. The Virgo tendency to worry, especially about matters of health, could lead to an air of hypochondria in the home. However, Virgo quick thinking and wit can usually overcome these disadvantages.

VIRGO AT WORK

At work, the person who has a typical Virgo personality will exhibit the following characteristics.

Typical behaviour and abilities

A typical Virgo at work
- is best in a supporting role
- is meticulous and self-disciplined
- offers others a sense of stability
- is very helpful to other people
- can enjoy complicated, routine work

Virgo as employer

A typical Virgo boss (male or female)
- is excellent as boss of a small company
- can see the details very clearly
- will call a spade a spade
- expects honesty in all matters
- is kind-hearted, honest and fair
- expects good grooming, good manners and good habits

- can handle extremely complicated projects
- will reward good work with pay not perks

Virgo as employee

A typical Virgo employee (male or female)
- is good in service work or research, rather than manufacturing
- will become an excellent assistant to the boss
- does good work and expects correct pay
- is courteous, reliable and thorough
- is quick-thinking, analytical and intelligent
- will be cautious, critical and methodical

Working environment

The workplace of a typical Virgo man or woman
- will not be noisy
- will have the most up-to-date equipment
- is best decorated with subtle, neutral colours
- is organized so that work can have a regular routine

Typical occupations

Any occupation which enables the Virgoan to give service and handle complicated or difficult details will suit most Virgoans.

VIRGO AND LOVE

To Virgo, love is not dramatic, emotional or sentimental. A Virgo's love is devotion and will include love of family, friends and those less fortunate than he or she. Virgo in love with another person will have many of the characteristics listed below.

Behaviour when in love

The typical Virgo

- looks for quality
- is frightened by overt romance
- may wait for years for the right person
- once in love, loves warmly and steadily
- is devoted to the loved one
- will rarely give cause for any jealousy
- will do anything to avoid breaking up

Expectations

The typical Virgo expects

- devotion from the partner
- a sense of decency
- to enjoy platonic flirtation
- to be fussed over when feeling down
- personal matters to be kept private
- feelings to be handled with great care

The end of an affair

Virgos are typically loyal and will avoid ending a marriage or other permanent relationship whenever possible. However, in the long run, Virgos are sensible, practical people. If the Virgoan sense of fair play has been outraged, the Virgo will make a quick and final break, legally and in every other way.

It is rare for a typical Virgo to linger in a fading marriage. If sensible, intelligent discussion does not solve the problems, the Virgo soon makes up his or her mind to end it.

Reconciliation is not typical of Virgoan behaviour. Pleading, tears, sentimentality or a more aggressive approach will have no effect. Because the Virgoan has good self-discipline, the past is soon put aside. However, if children are involved, the Virgo divorcé or divorcée will want to ensure the children are properly educated.

VIRGO AND SEX

When a typical Virgo makes love it is a pure-minded, natural, healthy act. Virgo only enjoys sex when it is with someone who has gained Virgo's confidence.

Celibacy, for short or long periods, is not usually difficult for a Virgo. In general, Virgoans are looking for a spouse, not a one-night-stand or an affair.

A Virgo who has not had his or her fragile sense of self undermined in youth will enjoy sex. The bedside library may include informative books on sex, because Virgos like to understand the finer details.

Virgo (male or female) tends to seduce with finesse, charm and subtlety.

The fact that typical Virgoan instincts are chaste does not mean that Virgos are virgins. The Virgin of astrology is a symbol of self-improvement and fertility.

VIRGO AND PARTNER

The person who contemplates becoming the marriage or business partner of a typical Virgo must realize that Virgo will regard the union as permanent, although the finer details can be flexible.

Given this, the person who partners Virgo can expect absolute loyalty. Virgos make strong commitments because they combine duty with devotion.

The Virgo will approach a proposal with great caution and will analyse the pros and cons thoroughly before getting involved. This is an excellent approach to any long-term partnership but may sound rather cold and clinical in the case of a proposed marriage.

Virgo man as partner

He will be thoughtful, considerate and honest. He will remember dates, anniversaries and agreements. He can be a wizard when it comes to the sensible balancing of the budget. He will love, honour and criticize, but will not expect to be obeyed, waited on or be dazzled by sexy make-up and clothes. However, he will want cleanliness and a lot of warmth and sincere respect.

Virgo woman as partner

She is shy but as tough as nails when the need arises. In business she will be cool, intelligent and fully committed.

Slow to love, Virgo woman is not interested in anything less than true love. When it happens, she will love intensely. She will only break a partnership if there has been hypocrisy. She is the most practical romantic in the zodiac.

Opposite sign

Pisces is the complementary opposite sign to Virgo. From Pisces, Virgo can learn to let go a little and float with the tide, giving imagination a chance to develop. In this way, Virgo can begin to accept human imperfections, especially his or her own.

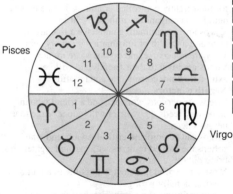

Pisces

Virgo

VIRGO AND FRIENDS

In general Virgo likes a friend who is tidy, clean and intelligent with a broad range of interests. They prefer people who are not given to big shows of emotion and are attracted to those who offer a sense of peace and serenity.

Positive factors

Virgos love any pageantry that gives them an outlet for their tightly controlled emotions. Hence they are delightful companions at these events.

Virgos are discriminating and have a fine artistic taste and a wealth of information on many subjects. They are not coarse and do not waste money.

Virgos are loyal to their friends and will be extremely kind, considerate and helpful.

Negative factors

Virgos are nervous worriers, and a friend who in some way feeds the worries will reduce Virgo to a nervous heap.

Virgos can be cold and critical, so a friend who softens the barbed remarks with caring laughter will bring out the Virgo wit.

Most Virgos find it almost impossible to admit they are occasionally wrong.

A compatibility chart, opposite, lists those with whom Virgo is likely to have the most satisfactory relationships.

Compatibility chart
In general, if people are typical of their zodiac sign, relationships between Virgo and other signs (including the complementary opposite sign, Pisces) are as shown below

	Harmonious	Difficult	Turbulent
Virgo	●		
Libra	●		
Scorpio	●		
Sagittarius		●	
Capricorn	●		
Aquarius			●
Pisces		●	
Aries			●
Taurus	●		
Gemini		●	
Cancer	●		
Leo	●		

VIRGOAN LEISURE INTERESTS

Most Virgos enjoy intellectual and practical pursuits. While many will take regular exercise for the sake of their health, they are not natural sportsmen and women.

Virgoan likes and dislikes

Likes

- making lists
- a well-stocked medicine cupboard
- self-inprovement courses
- punctuality
- mimicking others
- grooming self, taking showers, lovely soaps
- attending to the finest details
- very small animals, even ants
- being of service to others
- sensible, tailored clothes
- muted, subtle colours and textures

Dislikes

- crowds and noise; brash people
- slang, vulgarity, slovenliness and dirt
- people who whine and complain a lot
- sitting still for a long time
- disrupted schedules
- lids left off boxes, tins or toothpaste
- being under an obligation
- people who move Virgo's personal things
- hypocrisy and deceit
- any admission of weakness or failure
- bright, bold, primary colours

On the whole, typical Virgos pursue the following
leisure interests:

- theatre, concerts, plays, pageants
- books, magazines, dictionaries, encyclopaedias
- detailed crafts, especially weaving
- cults, alternative medicines, psychology
- gardening, health foods, flowers
- computers with all the paraphernalia

 VIRGOAN HEALTH

Typical Virgos are healthy although, if
very worried or unhappy, they may
succumb to the Virgoan tendency
towards hypochondria.

Types of sickness

Diseases most usually associated with Virgo are
disturbances of the lymph system, or the digestive
system such as appendicitis, malnutrition, diarrhoea,
indigestion, hernia etc. Normally Virgos look after
themselves well, so avoiding many upsets.

When Virgo is ill, he or she needs to have a little
fuss made while being encouraged to get well.

Virgo at rest

Extending the metaphor of Virgo as the mutable
earth sign, it follows that adaptability (the mutable
quality) can sometimes work for Virgo, who finds it
easy to change position if the body or mind are
under stress. However, Virgo is also nervously
restless, so Virgo needs plenty of interesting,
practical things to keep him or her occupied. Making
detailed models or doing needlework can be very
soothing and relaxing.

Parts of the body linked to Virgo
Traditionally, the parts of the body linked with a strong Virgo influence are as shown in the diagram below. Only the individual birthchart will show if one or more of these parts of the body have inherited a strength or a vulnerability. Any generalization would be misleading.

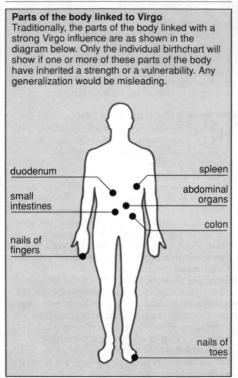

duodenum

spleen

abdominal organs

small intestines

colon

nails of fingers

nails of toes

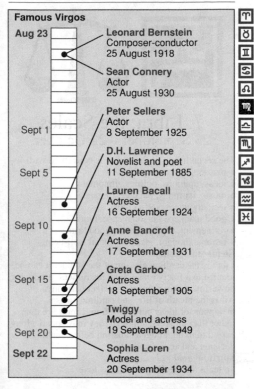

Famous Virgos

Aug 23

Leonard Bernstein
Composer-conductor
25 August 1918

Sean Connery
Actor
25 August 1930

Peter Sellers
Actor
8 September 1925

Sept 1

D.H. Lawrence
Novelist and poet
11 September 1885

Sept 5

Lauren Bacall
Actress
16 September 1924

Sept 10

Anne Bancroft
Actress
17 September 1931

Sept 15

Greta Garbo
Actress
18 September 1905

Twiggy
Model and actress
19 September 1949

Sept 20

Sophia Loren
Actress
20 September 1934

Sept 22

7. Libra: the Scales
23 September – 22 October

The seventh sign of the zodiac is concerned with
- partnership, relationships
- ideas, opinions, politics, diplomacy
- music, harmony, balance, romance
- tact, argument, self-control
- good manners, personal appearance
- refinement, sophistication, good taste
- rational thought, ideas for social well-being

Elemental quality

Libra is the cardinal air sign of the zodiac. It can be likened to a finely tuned wind instrument, producing powerful, moving music in perfect harmony.

Air is the breath of life, and cardinal air is a metaphor for ideas put into action. Libras are doers rather than thinkers, although they may spend a long period thinking about a situation before making a decision and acting upon it.

Spiritual goal

To learn the meaning of selfless love.

THE LIBRAN PERSONALITY

These are the general personality traits found in people who are typical of Libra. An unhappy or frustrated Libra may display some of the not-so-attractive traits.

Characteristics

Positive	Negative
• Cooperative	• Narcissistic
• Good companion	• Indolent or sulky
• Artistic	• Fearful
• Refined	• Indecisive
• Has clear opinions	• Manipulative
• Good negotiator	• Overbearing
• Very strong beliefs	• Flirtatious
• Loving and romantic	
• Sense of fair play	
• Able to lead on behalf of good causes	
• Uses intellect when going into action	
• Sincere	
• Charming	
• Communicative	
• An excellent mediator	

Secret Libra

Inside anyone who has strong Libran influences is a person who is terrified of being alone. The fear is usually well controlled so the typical Libra always

looks calm, collected and in charge of the situation.
Good-natured and loving, Libras can also be
petulant, and even objectionable, when asked to take
orders. Similarly, they are extremely intelligent, yet
sometimes gullible; they enjoy talking to people, yet
can also be very attentive listeners.

The Libra symbol (the scales) is a clue to
understanding this apparent inconsistency in
behaviour. In the attempt to gain an even balance,
the scales first tip one way and then the other. This
is how the typical Libra behaves – constantly trying
to attain that perfect balance.

Ruling planet and its effect

Venus rules the zodiac sign of Libra, so anyone
whose birthchart has a strong Libran influence will
tend to be a gentle, loving, peacemaker – until the
scales tip too far and need to be adjusted.

In astrology, Venus is the planet of values, self,
possessions, beauty and love. Libras tend to express
these attributes in words and action.

Libran lucky connections	
Colours	green, purple, pink
Plants	aloe, myrtle, rose
Perfume	galbanum
Gemstone	emerald
Metal	copper
Tarot card	justice
Animal	elephant

THE LIBRAN LOOK

People who exhibit the physical characteristics distinctive of the sign of Libra are not easy to describe, since there is no typical Libran feature, except for the dimple. It is a Libran habit to spend time deciding what to wear each morning, and to change clothes during the day if the occasion demands it.

Physical appearance
- Features are generally well balanced
- Face is pleasant, even when angry
- There may be a dimple in the chin, or in the cheeks or knees
- Charming smile

THE LIBRA MALE

If a man behaves in a way typical of the personality associated with the zodiac sign of Libra, he will have a tendency towards the characteristics listed below, unless there are influences in his personal birthchart that are stronger than that of his Libra sun sign.

Appearance
The typical Libra man
- is usually handsome, but is never ugly
- has a fine bone structure and balanced features
- has a clear and very charming voice
- dresses with discrimination in subtle colours
- is usually graceful and athletic
- likes to check his appearance in mirrors or as he passes a shop window

Behaviour and personality traits

The typical Libra man

- is very keen to make a visual impression that is appropriate to the task in hand, whether it be an international conference, a romantic assignation or a day on the beach
- gives advice freely
- is interested in the opposite sex, at all ages
- is a master in the art of romance
- is very trustworthy
- can be fickle and change his mind often
- is interested in the facts of a situation so that he can come to a balanced decision
- enjoys art and needs harmony
- can be lavish with money, spending it on things that will bring happiness
- has financial abilities

 THE LIBRA FEMALE

If a woman behaves in a way that is distinctive of the personality associated with the zodiac sign of Libra, she will have a tendency towards the characteristics listed below, provided there are no influences that are stronger than her Libra sun sign.

Appearance

The typical Libra woman

- is usually slim but curvy
- has large eyes
- has delicately flared nostrils
- has a large, well-shaped mouth
- has even teeth, often a gap between the front two

Behaviour and personality traits
The typical Libra woman
- is very aware of her looks
- takes care of her body and appearance
- uses her natural attraction to get what she wants
- presents her opinions with diplomacy and tact
- is excellent at partnership and teamwork
- loves luxurious clothes and perfumes
- has excellent powers of analysis
- will create a beautiful home

YOUNG LIBRA

If a child behaves in a way that is distinctive of the personality associated with the zodiac sign of Libra, he or she will have a tendency towards the characteristics listed below.

Behaviour and personality traits
The typical Libra child
- is a really beautiful baby
- hates having to decide between two things
- does not like to be hurried
- is fond of sweets
- always seems to know more about things than seems likely for someone of that particular age
- is kind-hearted
- likes to be fair and to be treated fairly
- can wheedle almost anything out of adults
- will obey rules if they are seen to be fair
- is usually neat and clean
- teenage Libras are romantics; they love warm water, bubble baths and lazy days in the sunshine

Bringing up young Libra
Most young Libras quickly learn how to argue about
everything with total conviction. They use this
natural ability to make their needs and wants
known. It is difficult for a parent to avoid complying
with such reasonable, fair-minded demands. To
always give in is to risk spoiling young Libra. But to
refuse their requests too often may injure the child's
developing sensibilities – so the parents of a Libra
need to keep their wits about them and aim for a
balance in these matters.

Young Libra's needs A harmonious environment
and fair treatment are essential to the developing
Libra. Privacy is regarded as sacred. Similarly, Libra
will respect the privacy of others and will keep
confidences.

Affection and, especially, attention are crucial.
While Libras can pursue their interests alone,
however, they also need company. It is from close
contact with others that they learn who they are.

What to teach young Libra At a very early age,
young Libra needs to be given direction and told,
gently and firmly, what to do and when to do it.
What may appear to be reluctance to do something
is often a sign that young Libra is giving extensive
thought to the matter in hand.

Most young Libras seem to know more about
everything than anyone else. This can be irritating,
especially when they are right. Parents need to take
an optimistic view of this tendency, and should
provide plenty of sound information. Young Libra
absorbs information readily from books.

Libras do not usually need to be strongly
disciplined, as they are good at disciplining
themselves. But it is important not to spoil them or
fuss over them too much, or they will become
impossible to handle and make their own and
everyone else's life a misery.

LIBRA AT HOME

If a person has the personality that is
typical of those born with a Libra sun
sign, home is a place to retire to for rest
and recuperation, ready for the next period of
sustained activity. The Libra will have a tendency
towards the characteristics listed below.

Typical behaviour and abilities

When at home, a Libra man or woman

- will spend time just lounging around listening to
  music or reading pleasant books
- will enjoy arguing about almost everything with
  all the family – just for the sake of it
- uses good taste to create a place of harmony
- will be a very gracious host, offering good food
  and wines while making interesting conversation
- will keep the place tidy and clean, unless he or she
  has become resentful due to unfair treatment.

Libra as parent

The typical Libra parent

- is often quite permissive
- may spoil the children
- likes to be proud of the children's appearance
  and behaviour
- will show his or her children much affection

- gives the children the best possible education
- will try to be just and fair
- will probably dominate the family

Two Libras in the same family

Two Libras are likely to understand each other's need for a peaceful, pleasant home. Providing they both have similar tastes in music, life will be smooth, although their other interests may be different. If there are children, they may eventually follow very different careers. Two Libras may be quite convinced that they are not at all alike. Anyone listening to them saying this will actually be struck by how similar they are. Libran twins will be extremely attached to each other, although one will usually tend to dominate the other.

LIBRA AT WORK

At work, the person who has a typical Libran personality will exhibit the following characteristics.

Typical behaviour and abilities

A typical Libra at work
- takes time to get things right
- is usually honest in business
- is more often than not in a partnership
- is a great promoter of ideas
- builds a good network of contacts

Libra as employer

A typical Libra boss (male or female)
- is unhurried but extremely restless
- takes note of everyone's opinion before making decisions

- often suggests unusual answers to problems
- is an expert at the rational analysis of situations
- believes his or her policy is the best
- has strong opinions about finance

Libra as employee

A typical Libra employee (male or female)

- belongs to a union
- expects and gives a fair deal
- never gossips, although he or she talks a lot
- mediates effectively in personality tiffs
- can be moody, but is not nasty
- needs periods of rest

Working environment

The workplace of a typical Libra man or woman

- must be harmonious – Libras can get migraines just because the walls are the wrong colour
- should be peaceful
- if there is music, it must be classical or refined
- should be free from anything upsetting
- will have a calm but purposeful atmosphere

Typical occupations

Libra is liable to be involved with any aspect of the law, politics or diplomacy. Their eye for design may lead them into areas such as fashion, art dealership, or graphics. They will also enjoy working in jobs that involve talking and presentation, such as promotional work. Many Libras are good at planning business ventures.

LIBRA AND LOVE

To Libra, love is all. He or she tends to fall in love with love itself, and is eager to share life with the partner. The Libran ideal is a life that is filled with the peaceful, rosy glow of romance. Libra in love will have many of the characteristics listed below.

Behaviour when in love

The typical Libra

- is emotionally dependent upon the partner
- is casual and easy-going
- enjoys romantic settings
- will ignore the partner's shortcomings in return for love
- does not want a partner who is overly demonstrative
- glows with love for the whole world
- will do anything to avoid hurting the loved one
- gives the loved one complete attention

Expectations

The typical Libra expects

- to be supported and cared for
- faithfulness and loyalty
- to be free to get on with his or her work
- a partner to have his or her own separate interests
- to be amused
- to be admired and even exalted

The end of an affair

If a Libra is rejected, he or she is initially demoralized. However, the Libra quickly takes action to try to redress the balance that has been lost. Often the Libra will do everything to charm the

loved one again, courting the partner as if for the
first time.
If the rejection is final, the hurt Libra will disguise
the pain he or she feels by searching once more for
true love.
A Libra is most likely to reject a partner who makes
too many demands on the Libran emotions. If this
happens, the break will be as orderly and as well-
mannered as possible.

♀♂ **LIBRA AND SEX**
When a typical Libra makes love it is not
always a passionate experience, unless
there are more passionate signs in the
Libra's chart.
Libras may appear to be calm, confident and in
control, but they are often very uncertain about their
sexual identity. They are usually very influenced by
images of sexual attractiveness in the media, and no
matter how beautiful or handsome they are (and
they often are) Libras can feel sexually very
insecure and uncertain. All this does not, however,
lessen Libra's interest in sex.

 LIBRA AND PARTNER
The person who contemplates becoming
the marriage or business partner of a
typical Libra must realize that Libra
forms partnerships to avoid the terrible sense of
loneliness which is ever present at the heart of a
Libra.
Given this, the person who partners Libra can expect

the marriage or the business to be happy and successful. Libra is the zodiac sign of partnerships, and typical Libras cannot imagine life without a relationship. The Libra will work hard and thoughtfully to make the partnership a harmonious balance of two personalities.

Libra man as partner

He will want a partner who has some good social or business connections. The young or immature Libra sees himself as the ugly duckling of the fairy tale. He will want his partner to be his personal mirror, reflecting back to him a self-image that is mature and confident. The developed Libra will indeed grow into a swan, but most Libras need plenty of encouragement on the way.

In a partnership, Libra will generally take charge of the finances, making sure that there is always a good bank balance. Libras tend to have very strong views about money.

Libra woman as partner

The young, inexperienced Libran female will see a partner as the provider of all that she needs. As she matures, she will want to share herself with her partner. She will have plenty of talent and energy, and her aim is to be successful in every field.

She will bring logic and sophistication to any business and a calm beauty to her home – where she will help her loved one to relax and to be renewed.

Opposite sign

Aries is the complementary opposite sign to Libra. Although relations between them can be difficult, they can become entirely complementary to each other as they mature. Aries, the sign of self, can inspire Libra to take the initiative alone sometimes. Libra can thus learn to become self-sufficient, and also gain a greater sense of personal identity. In this way, Libra, the sign of partnership, may be able to enjoy a separate identity while in a partnership.

LIBRA AND FRIENDS

Libras are usually very social people who like to be on the go. Life for Libras revolves around keeping in touch with other people; this is what makes them happy.

Libras will work hard for a friend, giving of themselves tirelessly for days on end. When they become tired, they will need to rest completely. But friends should not mistake the Libran recuperation periods as a loss of interest.

Positive factors

Libras are loving friends, and are unlikely to embarrass anyone with emotional outbursts. A Libran friend is honest and will treat a friend fairly. They make sensitive companions for visits to events concerned with the arts.

Negative factors

Libras can occasionally try the patience of a friend by their indecisiveness.

They can be jealous of a friend who is better looking than he or she is.

Friends must also be aware of the periodical depressive moods into which Libras seem to plunge. Such moods can be lightened by a genuine compliment.

Friends should never forget that the worst thing for a Libra is to be left alone for too long. If this happens they can become irritable, sulky and very low in self-esteem.

A compatibility chart, opposite, lists those with whom Libra is likely to have the most satisfactory relationships.

Compatibility chart
In general, if people are typical of their zodiac sign, relationships between Libra and other signs (including the complementary opposite sign, Aries) are as shown below

	Harmonious	Difficult	Turbulent
Libra	●		
Scorpio	●		
Sagittarius	●		
Capricorn		●	
Aquarius	●		
Pisces			●
Aries		●	
Taurus			●
Gemini	●		
Cancer		●	
Leo	●		
Virgo	●		

LIBRAN LEISURE INTERESTS
Most typical Libras are not over-fond of vigorous, sweaty exercise. This offends their preference for a harmony of the senses. Whatever exercise they take, it must enable them to stay relatively neat and unruffled. Many Libras have a lasting interest in the arts. Of these, music is a high priority.

Libran likes and dislikes

Likes

- pleasing surroundings
- getting notes, cards and flowers
- a good, detailed argument
- being fussed over
- being admired
- people running errands for them
- credit cards and store cards
- having people around
- attending to the finest details
- very small animals, even ants
- being of service to others
- sensible, tailored clothes
- muted, subtle colours and textures

Dislikes

- loud arguments
- confused situations
- sloppiness, especially in public
- ugly places
- being pressured to make up their mind
- being told it is up to them to make a change
- any criticism of their chosen partner or project

On the whole, typical Libras pursue the following leisure interests:

- listening to music, studying music history, playing an instrument in a group, such as a string quartet or a jazz band, listening to poetry
- dancing, especially graceful styles
- dressing with sophistication
- eating out in romantic settings
- the scientific side of cooking
- computers
- any kind of discussion group

LIBRAN HEALTH

Typical Libras have a tendency to become ill if they are obliged to live or work alone for long periods. Otherwise Libras are generally healthy people, and recover from any medical problem very quickly when they are in beautiful, calm surroundings.

Types of sickness

Back problems are typical, and any disease of the kidneys, liver and skin. Whatever the physical problem, a Libra puts on a brave face in public and will respond very positively to a lot of fuss and attention from their loved ones and friends.

The Libra at rest

A typical Libra loves a luxurious bedroom where they can lie around in blissful indolence. While at rest, the Libran mind is rarely still, but is planning ahead.

Parts of the body linked to Libra

Traditionally, the parts of the body linked with a strong Libra influence are as shown in the diagram below. Only the individual birthchart will show if one or more of these parts of the body have inherited a strength or a vulnerability. Any generalization would be misleading.

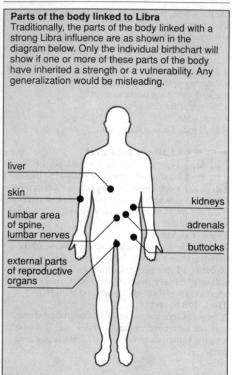

liver

skin

lumbar area
of spine,
lumbar nerves

external parts
of reproductive
organs

kidneys

adrenals

buttocks

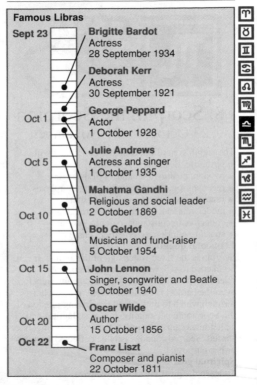

Famous Libras

Sept 23 — **Brigitte Bardot**
Actress
28 September 1934

Deborah Kerr
Actress
30 September 1921

Oct 1 — **George Peppard**
Actor
1 October 1928

Julie Andrews
Actress and singer
1 October 1935

Oct 5 — **Mahatma Gandhi**
Religious and social leader
2 October 1869

Oct 10 — **Bob Geldof**
Musician and fund-raiser
5 October 1954

Oct 15 — **John Lennon**
Singer, songwriter and Beatle
9 October 1940

Oscar Wilde
Author
15 October 1856

Oct 20

Oct 22 — **Franz Liszt**
Composer and pianist
22 October 1811

8. Scorpio: the Scorpion
23 October – 21 November

The eighth sign of the zodiac is concerned with
- birth, life, death, sex, sensuality
- passion, pushing boundaries of discovery
- regeneration, transformation, metamorphosis
- finance, investments, wills, inheritance
- hidden matters, secrets, taboos, magic
- collective unconscious, defence systems
- social revolution, reformation, change

Elemental quality

Scorpio is the fixed water sign of the zodiac. It can
be likened to still waters that run deep. The
relentless power of water to penetrate and transform
even the hardest rocks is an excellent metaphor
through which to understand the driving passion of
the Scorpionic personality. Just as stalagtites and
stalagmites cannot be prevented from growing, once
started, Scorpio cannot easily be deflected from his
or her purpose.

Spiritual goal

To learn the meaning of selfless love.

THE SCORPIONIC PERSONALITY

These are the general personality traits found in people who are typical of this sign. An unhappy or frustrated Scorpio may display some of the not-so-attractive traits.

Characteristics

Positive	Negative
• Self-critical	• Self-destructive
• Penetrating	• Ruthless
• Investigative	• Overbearing
• Passionately caring	• Suspicious
• Protective	• Jealous
• Tenacious	• Possessive
• Magnetic	• Dangerous
• Dynamic	• Quick-tempered
• Probing	• Obstinate
• Emotional	• Moody
• Sensual	• Sadistic
• Compassionate	• Insulting
• Concerned	• Secretive
• Unshockable	• Intolerant
• Intense	• Cunning
concentration	• Vindictive
• Understands failings	

Secret Scorpio

Inside anyone who has strong Scorpionic influences is a person who is intractable and impenetrable, so the secret Scorpio usually remains a secret. All

Scorpios like to keep their true nature as hidden as possible. Astrologically, a Scorpio is said to be at one or other of three stages of evolution.

A 'stage one' Scorpio exercises power through emotion and instinct. This Scorpio is symbolized by the scorpion, an insect more likely, in the end, to sting itself than others.

The 'stage two' type exercises power through the intellect. This Scorpio is symbolized by the golden eagle – a bird that soars higher than any other.

At the final stage of evolution, Scorpio exercises power through love. This Scorpio is symbolized by the dove of peace.

Ruling planet and its effect

Both Mars and Pluto rule the zodiac sign of Scorpio, so anyone whose birthchart has a strong Scorpio influence will tend to have two drives – one influenced by the battling energy of Mars and the other by the hidden depths of Pluto. In astrology, Mars is the planet of aggression and Pluto is the planet of magnetic forces.

Scorpionic lucky connections	
Colours	deep red, blue-green
Plants	cactus, ivy, oak
Perfume	Siamese benzoin
Gemstones	turquoise, snakestone, ruby
Metals	iron, steel
Tarot card	Death (regeneration)
Animals	wolf, grey lizard

THE SCORPIONIC LOOK

People who exhibit the physical characteristics distinctive of the sign of Scorpio have eyes that look at the world with almost hypnotic intensity. Eye colour and shape can vary widely, but if someone looks at you with deep penetration it is a sign of a personality strongly influenced by Scorpio.

Physical appearance

- broad face with wide forehead and thick neck
- strongly built body of middle stature
- generally slender with broad shoulders
- intense eyes

THE SCORPIO MALE

If a man behaves in a way typical of the personality associated with the zodiac sign of Scorpio, he will have a tendency towards the characteristics listed below, unless there are influences in his personal birthchart that are stronger than that of his Scorpio sun sign.

Appearance

The typical Scorpio man

- has strong features
- has penetrating eyes
- has thick eyebrows
- has hairy arms and legs
- has a well-proportioned figure
- has an athletic body
- has a tendency towards bow-legs

Behaviour and personality traits

The typical Scorpio man

- is never self-effacing
- is possessive of what he believes belongs to him
- has to maintain his dignity
- is a law unto himself and is most courageous in adversity
- will give absolutely honest advice, appraisal or compliments
- will move mountains to help someone
- is intensely loyal to friends
- never forgets a kindness, or an injury
- can be a saint or a sinner, but pursues either course with great zeal

 THE SCORPIO FEMALE

If a woman behaves in a way that is distinctive of the personality associated with the zodiac sign of Scorpio, she will have a tendency towards the characteristics listed below, providing there are no influences in her personal birthchart that are stronger than that of her Scorpio sun sign.

Appearance

The typical Scorpio woman

- has a compact and well-proportioned body
- has legs that are often short and thick
- is slender, but has a rather thick waist
- has attractive looks, even when frowning
- inclines her head downwards even when looking intensely at a person

Behaviour and personality traits

The typical Scorpio woman
- is poised and apparently cool
- never uses flattery
- only smiles when she means it
- wants total freedom of action
- regards flirting and flattery as insulting
- wants to dominate but can accept some restriction in order to win through in the end
- has many talents, all used with passion
- is loyal to family and home
- sets, and keeps to, her own standards

YOUNG SCORPIO

If a child behaves in a way that is distinctive of the personality associated with the zodiac sign of Scorpio, he or she will have a tendency towards the characteristics listed below.

Behaviour and personality traits

The typical Scorpio child
- enjoys a good fight and intends to win
- will learn only from a person seen as stronger
- keeps his or her own thoughts secret
- can find out everyone else's secrets easily
- has an instinctive understanding of adult problems
- can often bear pain well
- will be loving and loyal to family and friends
- will take revenge on others who break his/her favourite toys
- knows what he/she wants and goes out to get it
- is suspicious of strangers

Bringing up young Scorpio
Scorpio children are usually active, quick to learn
and intelligent. They have a passionate curiosity
which needs satisfying. They should be tactfully
guided away from too much interest in forbidden
areas, as they are fascinated by anything that is
hidden, mysterious or a private part of someone
else's life!

The best way to love a Scorpio child is to always be
loyal and to make it possible for him or her to follow
an interest in science, medicine, magic, engineering,
sports and literature.

Young Scorpio's needs A private place is essential
for Scorpionic children – somewhere they can be
alone and undisturbed. It could be a room of their
own, or even just a cupboard. It might be a secret
hiding-place or a little box with a key. A secret
hiding-place gives the Scorpio child a sense of
security.

What to teach young Scorpio Understanding the
rights and needs of others is an important lesson for
young Scorpio. In this way Scorpio children learn to
forgive the hurts and mishaps of everyday life.

SCORPIO AT HOME
If a person has the personality that is
typical of those born with a Scorpio sun
sign, home is a place to be proud of and
he or she will have a tendency towards the following
characteristics.

Typical behaviour and abilities

When at home, a Scorpio man or woman

- makes the home self-contained
- is protective of children
- is gentle with the sick
- guards home territory jealously
- likes the home kept clean and orderly
- expresses good taste
- enjoys comfort

Scorpio as parent

The typical Scorpio parent

- is strict about rules
- demands high standards
- enjoys the children
- keeps the children busy
- takes the children out a great deal
- finds it hard to change viewpoints and to bridge the generation gap
- cares passionately about the family
- remains his or her child's friend throughout life

Two Scorpios in the same family

They will understand each other only too well. Two Scorpios means double the passion, and it is essential that both have the facilities to follow their own passionate interests, so that no jealousies arise. Two Scorpios can get on well, provided each has a space of his or her own that is private.

The greatest problems could arise from sexual jealousy if the two are of the same sex and age-group. However, in the final analysis, the Scorpionic loyalty to family will overcome all other problems.

♈ ♉ ♊ ♋ ♌ ♍ ♎ ♏ ♐ ♑ ♒ ♓

SCORPIO AT WORK

At work, the person who has a typical Scorpionic personality will exhibit the following characteristics.

Typical behaviour and abilities

A typical Scorpio at work
- will eventually know everyone's secrets
- will sense the moods of other people
- is indefatigable
- will excel as a team leader
- will appear to be calm in all situations

Scorpio as employer

A typical Scorpio boss (male or female)
- will demand total loyalty
- will do anything to help someone he/she likes
- will solve even the most difficult problems
- will never reveal the depth of his competitiveness
- confronts problems directly
- will be concerned and compassionate towards the workers' families, regarding them as part of the team

Scorpio as employee

A typical Scorpio employee (male or female)
- is self-motivated
- knows what he/she wants to achieve
- will take any amount of criticism from someone who has something he/she wants
- will accept failure as inevitable only when the odds are overwhelming
- is tenacious, intense and career-minded
- does not waste time and is not a clock-watcher

Working environment

The workplace of a typical Scorpio man or woman
- suggests an air of quiet confidence
- is usually tidy, or at least orderly
- contains nothing superfluous to the job
- contains equipment that helps Scorpio increase knowledge and undertake shrewd analysis

Typical occupations

Scorpios enjoy solving mysteries and penetrating the secrets of life. They love to get to the heart of any problem, human or mechanical.

They may be detectives, pathologists, surgeons, scientists, researchers, undertakers, sewage workers, insurers, market analysts, butchers, members of the armed services or pharmacists.

Any occupation which Scorpios feel is important and offers the opportunity to investigate and analyse complex problems will satisfy them. Scorpios can run a big business or a small enterprise as long as they feel that they are achieving something.

 SCORPIO AND LOVE

To Scorpio, love is an intensely passionate and enduring emotion that may be directed at one person only. Love is central to the life of the typical Scorpio, and inspires many of their ambitions and actions. Scorpio in love will have many of the following characteristics.

Behaviour when in love
The typical Scorpio
- is deeply attached to the loved one
- attracts the loved one like a magnet
- is possessive
- hides emotions in public
- keeps dependence on the loved one hidden
- is faithful when in love
- dominates the loved one
- remains true to his/her own feelings

Expectations
The typical Scorpio expects
- absolute faithfulness and loyalty
- demonstrative love
- no great emphasis on romance
- genuine tenderness
- acknowledgement of how lucky the loved one is to be party to Scorpio's secrets

The end of an affair
If a Scorpio has an affair, it is often because the sexual life within the marriage has gone badly wrong. Scorpios seem able to attract partners without much effort, and will take the upper hand from the start, so that ending an affair is an easy matter.

However, the Scorpio who is rejected is always very wounded and may want to take revenge. Some Scorpios immediately attempt to hurt their ex-partner. Others take their revenge in more subtle ways over a period of time. A rejected Scorpio is unlikely to forgive, and will never forget, the hurt.

SCORPIO AND SEX

When a typical Scorpio makes love it is an expression of all the pent-up passion that is hidden inside this most magnetic of personalities. Sex is an important element of life to a Scorpio.

Indeed, Scorpio is the zodiac sign that indicates the greatest interest in sexual matters.

As in other areas of their life, Scorpios are liable to be both inventive and single-minded – but for most Scorpios, sex is very much an expression of love.

SCORPIO AND PARTNER

The person who contemplates becoming the marriage or business partner of a typical Scorpio must realize that Scorpio will expect to dominate the partnership.

Given this, the person who partners Scorpio can expect unwavering loyalty, hard work and a passionate drive to suceed – whether in business or marriage.

Scorpio man as partner

In business, the Scorpio man will inevitably be in charge of the partnership and is most likely to have initiated the terms of agreement. A Scorpio who accepts orders from a partner is doing so for a particular reason. For example, if money or future progress are the reward, Scorpio will appear to accept even a subordinate position for as long as it takes to achieve the results he wants.

Scorpio will be proud of his partner and his partner's

skills, and will go out of his way to enable the
partner to achieve ambitions too.

Scorpio woman as partner

A Scorpio woman is often even more subtle than her
male counterpart. She happily accepts the
subordinate role and plays this part well. Again,
however, this is only so that she can achieve her
ambition in the end.

Like her male counterpart, she will be loyal to the
partner and do everything to help the partner.
Scorpios can work very hard and they often provide
the dynamism in a business.

It is unlikely that Scorpio and her partner will have
an equal footing. The Scorpio will, in reality, have
the edge on the partner – but only in ways that the
Scorpio sees will be helpful to the joint venture.
Scorpio shrewdness is a vital asset in any
partnership.

Opposite sign

Taurus is the complementary opposite sign to
Scorpio. From Taurus, Scorpio can learn to
recognize the talents of other people and appreciate
their value. In this way, Scorpio can learn to value
his or her own talents more realistically, because
Scorpio is more self-critical than critical of others,
and often reproaches him- or herself.

Opposite sign

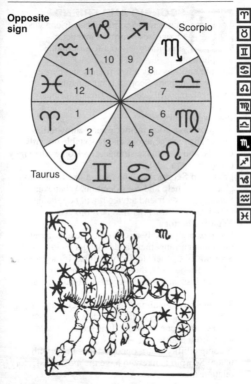

Scorpio

Taurus

SCORPIO AND FRIENDS

In general, Scorpio likes a friend who recognizes Scorpio's magnetic superiority without fear or undue compliments.

Scorpio chooses only a few friends and expects loyalty from them. Scorpio is not a natural socializer, but will keep close friends for many years.

Positive factors

Scorpios have good memories and enjoy telling jokes. They are generous and hospitable towards friends, and also make strangers welcome when they call for help or advice.

Friends of Scorpios will be treated like family and given every help and consideration. Whenever Scorpio gives a friend advice it will be reliable. A friend can also trust Scorpio never to gossip.

Negative factors

Scorpios are unlikely to call on a friend without making an arrangement and having a good reason. Scorpios like others to do the calling. If they are out when a friend calls, their attitude is that it is the friend's loss, and that the friend will have to call again.

Scorpios have an almost psychic insight into the motives and secrets of their friends. Anyone who dislikes someone knowing their secrets should stay away from Scorpios.

A compatibility chart, opposite, lists those with whom Scorpio is likely to have the most satisfactory relationships.

Compatibility chart
In general, if people are typical of their zodiac
sign, relationships between Scorpio and other
signs (including the complementary opposite
sign, Taurus) are as shown below

	Harmonious	Difficult	Turbulent
Scorpio	●		
Sagittarius	●		
Capricorn	●		
Aquarius		●	
Pisces	●		
Aries			●
Taurus		●	
Gemini			●
Cancer	●		
Leo		●	
Virgo	●		
Libra	●		

SCORPIONIC LEISURE INTERESTS

Finding out how things work, taking something to pieces and reconstructing it, or delving into the mysteries of the human mind are all of interest to Scorpios, who also enjoy a variety of sports. Winning is important to them.

On the whole, typical Scorpios pursue the following leisure interests:

- any sport that demands shrewd tactics
- competitive driving, flying, or cycling
- scientific hobbies
- archaeology, anthropology, psychology
- detective novels, treasure hunts, caving
- breeding animals or plants

Scorpionic likes and dislikes

Likes

• activity	• sex
• mysteries	• being acknowledged
• secrets	• home
• winning	

Dislikes

• being analysed	• too many
• being asked	compliments
personal questions	• having to trust a
• people who know	stranger
more than they do	

SCORPIONIC HEALTH

Typical Scorpios are rarely ill. When they do become sick it is generally serious, but they have the willpower to get well. Scorpios can destroy their own health by allowing themselves to get depressed or by doing too much hard work.

Types of sickness

Some Scorpios are prone to accidents due to their burning desire to finish a job or get somewhere more quickly than anyone else.

Nose and throat problems, hernias, piles, bladder disorders and problems with the reproductive organs are the most common Scorpio illnesses.

The phoenix symbolizes Scorpio's activities, and in matters of health it seems that Scorpio has a tremendous ability to rise from the metaphoric ashes of sickness and fly again.

Scorpio at rest

Scorpios often find it hard to relax. Some Scorpios will even avoid situations where they can relax. When taking a holiday, they often seem to have a small accident or minor illness in the first week. Many Scorpios try to relax by continuing to work because of the intense pressure they put on themselves to finish everything before leaving for that much needed rest. Their best policy is to have an alternative interest or hobby that they can pursue with passion, thus giving them relaxation from their main work. This especially applies to Scorpios who are housewives and mothers, as they may find it difficult to take even a short break.

Parts of the body linked to Scorpio
Traditionally, the parts of the body linked with a
strong Scorpio influence are as shown in the
diagram below. Only the individual birthchart will
show if one or more of these parts of the body
have inherited a strength or a vulnerability. Any
generalization would be misleading.

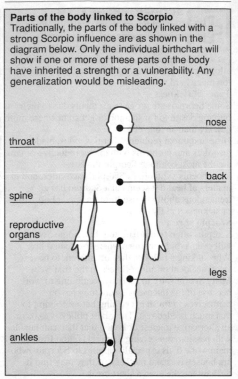

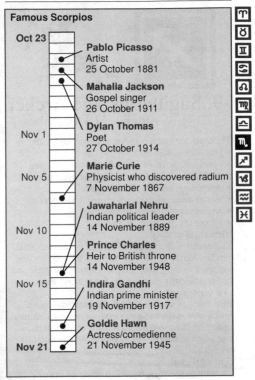

Famous Scorpios

Oct 23

Pablo Picasso
Artist
25 October 1881

Mahalia Jackson
Gospel singer
26 October 1911

Dylan Thomas
Poet
27 October 1914

Nov 1

Nov 5

Marie Curie
Physicist who discovered radium
7 November 1867

Jawaharlal Nehru
Indian political leader
14 November 1889

Nov 10

Prince Charles
Heir to British throne
14 November 1948

Nov 15

Indira Gandhi
Indian prime minister
19 November 1917

Goldie Hawn
Actress/comedienne
21 November 1945

Nov 21

9. Sagittarius: the Archer
22 November – 21 December

The ninth sign of the zodiac is concerned with
- philosophy, idealism, religion, spiritual growth
- optimism, positive outlook, forward planning
- travel, freedom of movement, the outdoors
- generosity, honesty, justice, morality
- imagination, aspirations, open-mindedness
- wit, intellect, flashes of intuition
- generosity, pleasure, romance

Elemental quality

Sagittarius is the mutable fire sign of the zodiac. It can be likened to stars, a thousand lighted candles, the sparks rising from a rapidly spreading grass fire, or the reflectors marking the route along the centre of a major road.

Fire changes substances and Sagittarians have a knack of transforming negative situations with their optimism. Mutable means adaptable. Sagittarians can adapt to almost any situation, whether earthly or spiritual.

Spiritual goal

To learn to use their talents to guide others.

THE SAGITTARIAN PERSONALITY

These are the general personality traits found in people who are typical of Sagittarius. An unhappy or frustrated Sagittarius may display some of the not-so-attractive traits.

Characteristics

Positive	Negative
• Frank and open	• Argumentative
• Optimistic	• Impatient to be
• Sees the best in people	moving
• Honest and fair-minded	• Critical of those who deny their talents
• Spiritual	• A gambler at heart
• Enthusiastic	• Can be a fanatic
• Inspiring	• Hot-headed
• Disarmingly happy	• Fails to plan adequately
• Stimulating	• Tends to preach
• Happy-go-lucky	• Denies sadness
• Holds no grudges	• Uncommitted
• Sensual	• Fears any responsibility that curtails freedom
	• Blundering and inept
	• Indulgent

Secret Sagittarius

Inside anyone who has strong Sagittarian influences is a person who wants to be free. Possessive partners, conservative thinkers, and bureaucrats that

Sagittarius comes into contact with should be aware of this.

No matter who or what the cause, the Sagittarian who is held back in life, in love or in opportunity for spiritual growth will be unhappy, even though he or she will keep smiling through all adversities.

Like the centaur, one of the Sagittarian symbols, the Sagittarian personality experiences conflict between mind and body. The Sagittarian purpose is to overcome this conflict so that they may guide others.

Ruling planet and its effect

Jupiter rules the zodiac sign of Sagittarius, so anyone whose birthchart has a strong Sagittarius influence will tend to be expansive, pleasure-loving, benevolent and have a strong sense of justice.

In astrology, Jupiter is the planet of beneficence. Psychologically, Jupiter is linked with wisdom and is the guide to the psyche.

Sagittarian lucky connections	
Colours	blue, royal blue, purple, white
Plants	rush, oak, fig, hyssop
Perfume	lignaloes
Gemstones	jacinth, lapis lazuli
Metal	tin
Tarot card	temperance
Animals	horse, dog

THE SAGITTARIAN LOOK

People who exhibit the physical characteristics distinctive of the sign of Sagittarius look strong and active. They are often taller than average and have handsome faces. Since a typical Sagittarius is an optimist, the face often appears about to break into a smile – and regularly does.

Physical appearance

- Body: strongly built and energetic; movement is normally quick, although not always graceful
- Head: large, well-shaped skull with a high, broad forehead
- Uses hands and arms to make broad, sweeping gestures
- Bright, intelligent and sparkling eyes which often twinkle with good humour
- Either tall and athletic in appearance, or shorter with a sturdier body. Excess weight can be a problem, as Sagittarius is ruled by expansive, jovial, life-loving Jupiter

THE SAGITTARIUS MALE

If a man behaves in a way typical of the personality associated with the zodiac sign of Sagittarius, he will have a tendency towards the characteristics listed below, unless there are influences in his personal birthchart that are stronger than that of his Sagittarius sun sign.

Appearance

The typical Sagittarius man

- can be likened to a lively horse, and often has a

mane of hair that falls over the forehead and has to
be tossed away. In later life the Sagittarius may
become bald, yet still retain a youthful look

- is physically noticeable, because of his strong
  sense of confidence
- will retain his physical faculties to a very old age

Behaviour and personality traits

The typical Sagittarius man

- is a risk-taker
- says exactly what is on his mind
- enjoys physical danger
- has an unerringly accurate wit
- has a good memory for facts, but often forgets
  where he has left everyday objects such as keys
- is trusting until let down
- can tell really funny jokes, but often fluffs the
  punchline – which makes the joke even funnier
- may be tactless but is never deliberately cruel
- likes learning, study and creative interpretation

 THE SAGITTARIUS FEMALE

If a woman behaves in a way that is
distinctive of the personality associated
with the zodiac sign of Sagittarius, she
will have a tendency towards the characteristics
listed below, providing there are no influences in her
personal birthchart that are stronger than that of her
Sagittarius sun sign.

Appearance

The typical Sagittarius woman

- has an oval face, a high forehead and a
  pointed chin

- has a tall and slender body
- has eyes that are steady, bright, open and honest
- has movement that is purposeful and even graceful

Behaviour and personality traits
The typical Sagittarius woman

- is honest
- enjoys freedom of thought and travel
- will laugh about her misfortunes and mistakes, even while she is upset or in pain
- is angry if her integrity is questioned
- is kind-hearted, though sometimes tactless
- can be deceived in romance, but is rarely misled in other areas of life
- enjoys taking risks, both physical and intellectual
- is often unconventional in relationships
- sticks by her own very clear moral standards
- can be cuttingly sarcastic when hurt
- regards herself and all others as equals

YOUNG SAGITTARIUS
If a child behaves in a way that is distinctive of the personality associated with the zodiac sign of Sagittarius, he or she will have a tendency towards the characteristics listed below.

Behaviour and personality traits
The typical Sagittarius child

- is a happy, playful little clown
- greets everyone and is despondent if others don't say 'Hello'
- acts on impulse

- is active, interested in many things and usually adores animals
- tends to get more bumps, bruises and cuts than many children because he or she is so adventurous, and rarely sits still
- gives and expects total honesty
- enjoys company
- when left on his or her own will hug a teddy or a blanket
- asks endless questions
- expects to be trusted

Bringing up young Sagittarius

Most young Sagittarians enjoy learning but dislike being held back by what they see as needless rules. They are capable of setting their own standards and should be encouraged to do so. A frustrated Sagittarian child can turn from being a happy-go-lucky optimist into an angry, sarcastic adult; therefore it is important that the child be allowed to take any opportunities for learning and socializing. Sagittarian children question adult values and poke fun at adult hypocrisy. The best thing that the parents of a Sagittarian can do is to be totally honest.

Young Sagittarius's needs Love is essential to all children, but the way it is given varies. In the case of young Sagittarius there should be no pressure or possessiveness, but love given by way of encouragement and by showing pleasure. Young Sagittarians hide their hurts, disappointments and sorrows behind a spirited belief that everything must get better. The clown who laughs while his heart is breaking is behaving in a very Sagittarian way.

What to teach young Sagittarius These restless, freedom-loving children need to be taught that there are some social rules that must be obeyed for their own good.

Handling money is another Sagittarian weakness, so a few practical lessons should be given: for example, not boosting pocket money that has been rashly spent. Economy does not come naturally to generous, expansive Sagittarians.

Wise parents will teach their Sagittarian offspring the facts of life from an early age, so that they are well-prepared when their adventures become romantic.

SAGITTARIUS AT HOME

If a person has the personality that is typical of those born with a Sagittarius sun sign, home is a place to rest the mind and body before moving off on the next trip. He or she will have a tendency towards the characteristics listed below.

Typical behaviour and abilities

When at home, a Sagittarius man or woman

- could be almost anywhere; Sagittarians make their home wherever they happen to be; some have, or would like, several homes, while others may be permanent travellers. It is not unusual for Sagittarians to spend time living abroad, or to divide their time between two different countries
- is usually planning for the next journey
- is not naturally domesticated
- enjoys making and receiving social calls

- does not enjoy formality, but loves informal
  gatherings where he/she is free to roam

Sagittarius as parent

The typical Sagittarius parent

- has very clear moral standards
- has faith in the children
- may expect too much intellectually
- will provide a very stimulating home
- will be eager to play with children, talk with them
  and take them on travels
- enjoys the children and is great fun as a parent
- will always answer questions honestly
- will encourage the children to leave home
  when grown up

Two Sagittarians in the same family

Sagittarians are not usually very good at family
relationships because they are natural wanderers and
resume contact sporadically. Hence, two typical
Sagittarians in the same family should get on
perfectly well; each will understand the other's need
for freedom of thought and action. Two Sagittarian
children are apt to get into more physical scrapes,
since they are both risk-takers.

SAGITTARIUS AT WORK

At work, the person who has a typical
Sagittarians personality will exhibit the
following characteristics.

Typical behaviour and abilities

A typical Sagittarian at work

- needs a challenge, so even in the dullest, most
  routine job, he or she will seek challenges

- is versatile
- needs to do several things at once
- may have two jobs
- needs intellectual and physical exercise
- gets tired only when bored

Sagittarius as employer

A typical Sagittarian boss (male or female)

- is rarely naturally tactful and may be quite blunt
- has a sense of overall planning, although they may overlook details
- expects people to be straightforward
- can be erratic and hard to tie down
- can promote anything extremely well
- can boost morale and will fight for what he/she believes is right
- is generally cheerful
- is kind and understanding

Sagittarius as employee

A typical Sagittarian employee (male or female)

- works best when allowed to get on with the job at their own speed – which is usually fast
- is cheerful and does not complain
- is enthusiastic, willing and generally ahead of everyone else
- enjoys praise and will promise almost anything
- is interested in current pay, but not in long-term career plans
- will boost everyone's spirits when they are downhearted

Working environment

The workplace of a typical Sagittarian man or woman

- is wherever they are – they take their tools with them
- will be open and airy
- may be decorated imaginatively

Typical occupations

Anything in sales and promotion that involves travel and knowledge of foreign languages; anything that allows Sagittarius to perform; and any career that involves learning and the use of the intellect such as teacher, barrister, or writer. A Sagittarius will be attracted to work that combines intellect and physical activity, such as veterinary practice, or indeed any kind of work with animals.

SAGITTARIUS AND LOVE

To Sagittarius, love is a romantic adventure. Sagittarius in love will have many of the characteristics listed below.

Behaviour when in love

The typical Sagittarius

- enjoys love on the move in foreign places
- is inventive
- needs good intellectual compatibility
- is totally honest with the loved one
- enjoys the physical pleasures of love
- is happy when he or she is loved
- is very generous and good humoured

Expectations

The typical Sagittarius expects

- not to be tied down
- to feel secure in love
- the loved one to be honest
- to retain freedom of movement
- to never be falsely accused of philandering
- to stimulate, amuse and be enjoyed by the loved one

The end of an affair

If a partner is possessive or jealous of Sagittarius, the relationship will begin to crack. Eventually, these pressures will cause Sagittarius to simply pack up and move on.

Sagittarians enjoy meeting people and may indulge in the occasional affair. On the whole, the attraction of the affair wil be its excitement, rather than true romance. Sagittarius is prone to look elsewhere if an existing relationship becomes routine.

SAGITTARIUS AND SEX

A typical Sagittarius regards love as another adventure to be enjoyed and explored. Sagittarians tend to take a chance on love, and they enter a relationship with the same recklessness that they display in other activities. In the relationship he or she will be warm and loving, and a wonderful companion.

Sagittarians normally enjoy a lot of touching and cuddling – a good, warm, loving hug is their form of security blanket. Common intellectual interests are equally essential to the success of any long-term sexual relationship.

SAGITTARIUS AND PARTNER

The person who contemplates becoming the marriage or business partner of a typical Sagittarius must realize that Sagittarius will value his or her freedom above everything. Given this, the person who partners Sagittarius can expect honesty and plenty of creative ideas.

Sagittarian man as partner

He will want a partner who enjoys spontaneity and who will appreciate his grand gestures and courageous outbursts of enthusiasm. He will also want a partner who will not try to control him.
In business, a person who has a sound understanding of financial matters would make the perfect partner.

Sagittarian woman as partner

Frank and friendly, she wants a partner who can love her for her outspoken charm, not wilt under it. Her words and actions will always show what she is thinking and feeling, so a potential partner should be quite clear about his own feelings. Sagittarian women are neither coy nor evasive, and will want a partner who does not play silly games. In marriage or in business, a partner must always ask her to do something, never tell her. However, she will respond to hints.

Opposite sign

Gemini is the complementary opposite sign to Sagittarius. Although relationships between the two may have some difficulties, Sagittarius can learn from Gemini how to notice and take account of details. In this way, Sagittarians can become inspiring guides, lighting the way for others, rather than leading them by preaching what the route should be.

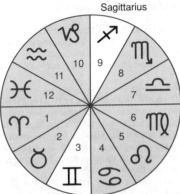
Sagittarius

Gemini

SAGITTARIUS AND FRIENDS

In general, Sagittarius likes a friend who is open-minded, ready for an adventure and trusting.

Positive factors

Sagittarians are friendly, gregarious people who accept any friend who matches up to their personal standards. They will defend a friend with great loyalty, but they will also say exactly what they think.

Sagittarians have friends from many walks of life.
Among those are likely to be both men and women,
straight and gay people, a range of ages and a
mixture of ethnic groups; they will all be treated as
equals.

Sagittarians respond to all calls for help. They will
lend a friend money without expecting it to be
repaid; they take in stray animals and stray people
and will support any cause in the name of
friendship.

Negative factors

Close friendship with just one or two people is not
the Sagittarian norm. In fact, anyone who tries to get
too familiar with, or who takes advantage of, the
Sagittarian natural friendliness, may be struck by the
fiery rocket of Sagittarian temper. They generally
fight with words, as sharp as darts, but some may
also use their fists.

Sagittarians can be eccentric, and may find it
difficult to keep a secret.

A compatibility chart, opposite, lists those with
whom Sagittarius is likely to have the most
satisfactory relationships.

SAGITTARIAN LEISURE INTERESTS

Sagittarians are versatile and like to kick
against authority, so their leisure interests
may be both varied and radical. Sports are natural
activities for Sagittarians, who enjoy them for the
social contact as much as for the competition.
A Sagittarian who has not travelled is unusual.

Compatibility chart

In general, if people are typical of their zodiac sign, relationships between Sagittarius and other signs (including the complementary opposite sign, Gemini) are as shown below.

	Harmonious	Difficult	Turbulent
Sagittarius	●		
Capricorn	●		
Aquarius	●		
Pisces		●	
Aries	●		
Taurus			●
Gemini		●	
Cancer			●
Leo	●		
Virgo		●	
Libra	●		
Scorpio	●		

Long-distance travel to foreign places is one of the main Sagittarian interests. Some may prefer to 'travel' in the world of literature or religion, but their travels will also be far and wide.

On the whole, typical Sagittarians pursue the following interests:

- gambling, gaming, racing cars, sky-diving and other risk-taking sports
- travel, exploration, cracking codes, tracking down mysteries, solving problems, speaking foreign languages, breeding animals, keeping pets
- religions, belief systems, new ways of being

Sagittarian likes and dislikes

Likes

- freedom of action
- alternative ideas
- being on the move
- food and drink
- perfumes and beauty aids
- raffles and lotteries
- parties, flirting

Dislikes

- disapproval from others
- making promises
- being too safe, secure or confined
- administration
- tight clothes
- having their honesty doubted

SAGITTARIAN HEALTH

Typical Sagittarians are healthy, energetic and able to keep going in adversity. They hate to be confined to bed, unless it is to dream a little; any kind of routine will tax the Sagittarian optimism. However, their positive outlook helps them to overcome illnesses quickly, and keeps them going if serious illness strikes.

Types of sickness

Diseases often linked with a Sagittarian influence in the chart are the whole range of arthritic and rheumatic problems, diseases that attack the hips and legs, and problems arising from the Sagittarian tendency to fall over, trip over or collide with things.

Asthma is linked with Sagittarius, as are sicknesses caught from animals – Sagittarians are very fond of animals and like to be closely involved with them. Sagittarians tend to take physical risks, so accidents arising from dangerous sports can be expected from time to time. The jovial Jupiter influence is said to lead many a Sagittarian into indulgence in food or drink, and this may lead to health problems.

Sagittarius at rest

A typical Sagittarian never rests. A Sagittarius who lounges around looking bored is one who feels restricted and needs to break free again. The way that typical Sagittarians rest is by sleeping, thinking and dreaming – and then moving off somewhere new.

Parts of the body linked to Sagittarius
Traditionally, the parts of the body linked with a strong Sagittarius influence are as shown in the diagram below. Only the individual birthchart will show if one or more of these parts of the body have inherited a strength or a vulnerability. Any generalization would be misleading.

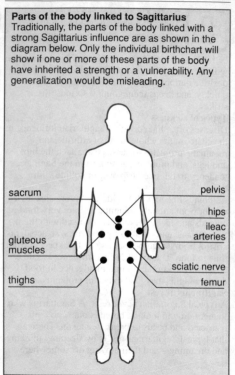

sacrum

pelvis

hips

ileac arteries

gluteous muscles

sciatic nerve

thighs

femur

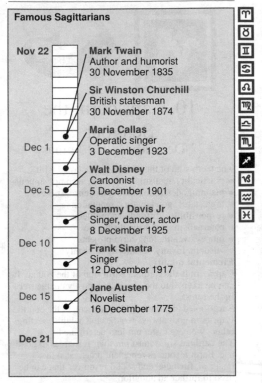

Famous Sagittarians

Nov 22

Mark Twain
Author and humorist
30 November 1835

Sir Winston Churchill
British statesman
30 November 1874

Maria Callas
Operatic singer
3 December 1923

Dec 1

Walt Disney
Cartoonist
5 December 1901

Dec 5

Sammy Davis Jr
Singer, dancer, actor
8 December 1925

Dec 10

Frank Sinatra
Singer
12 December 1917

Jane Austen
Novelist
16 December 1775

Dec 15

Dec 21

10. Capricorn: the Seagoat
22 December – 19 January

The tenth sign of the zodiac is concerned with
- practicality, realism, hard work, accomplishment
- planning, determination, persistence, success
- high status, good quality, reputation
- responsibility, difficulties, problems
- paternalism, authority, discipline
- money, wealth, long-term projects
- wisdom, loyalty, sensitivity to beauty

Elemental quality

Capricorn is the cardinal earth sign of the zodiac. It can be likened to the oldest and most valuable tree in the forest.

Sure-footed and thoroughly practical, in the end the Capricorn goat always reaches the heights, beating others who are faster but less determined.

The cardinal signs must put their resources to good use. Earth resources represent practical skills: material, financial and social resources that can be used to further an ambition.

Spiritual goal
To learn to understand the feelings and needs of
other people.

**THE CAPRICORNEAN
PERSONALITY**
These are the general personality traits
found in people who are typical of
Capricorn. An unhappy or frustrated Capricorn may
display some of the not-so-attractive traits.

Characteristics

Positive	Negative
• Good organizing skills	• Tendency to believe their way is always the best
• Cautious and realistic	• Egotistical
• Hard working	• A slave-driver
• Scrupulous	• Unforgiving
• Fearless	• Anxious, allows inner fears to dominate decisions
• Calculates risks but takes them when necessary	• Takes a very critical view
• Is an admiring spectator	• A perfectionist who is never satisfied
• Has high but realistic standards	• Fatalistic
• Conventional	• Status-seeking
• Concerned	
• Gives sound advice	
• Loyal to tradition	
• Respects authority	

Secret Capricorn

Inside anyone who has strong Capricornean influences is a person who worries about security – physical, social and emotional. A typical Capricorn cannot bear to be embarrassed in public. Sometimes, Capricorn longs to let go a little and to allow themselves to join in the fun – let their toes tap in time with the music. But usually a sense of duty and a terrible fear of looking foolish stop them from acting out their desires. Capricorns are also secret romantics who want a perfect and secure love in their lives.

Ruling planet and its effect

Saturn rules the zodiac sign of Capricorn, so anyone whose birthchart has a strong Capricornean influence will tend to take life seriously.

In astrology, Saturn is the planet of fate, time, sorrow, caution and wisdom. It is often called the great teacher, because Saturn is associated with the life-long task of gently working out our fears and overcoming them. Saturn is also the most beautiful of the planets.

Capricornean lucky connections	
Colours	green, black, grey, indigo, violet
Plants	yew, ash, hemp, weeping willow
Perfume	musk
Gemstones	jet, black diamond, onyx, ruby
Metal	lead
Tarot card	the devil
Animals	goat, ass

THE CAPRICORNEAN LOOK

People who exhibit the physical characteristics distinctive of the sign of Capricorn generally have a small skeletal structure. The shape of the body will depend on how well the musculature has been developed. If physical training is part of Capricorn's routine, then it will be done with determination and discipline, resulting in a well-developed musculature which may make a Capricorn look heavier than he or she really is.

A typical Capricorn has a serious look, and young Capricorns often look older than their years. It is also typical that ageing Capricorns eventually tend to become more relaxed and so look younger than their years.

Physical appearance

- Forehead: narrower than average between the temples, with deep frown lines
- Style of walking: swift and sure because all typical Capricorns take great care of where they put their feet when they take each step

THE CAPRICORN MALE

If a man behaves in a way typical of the personality associated with the zodiac sign of Capricorn, he will have a tendency towards the characteristics listed below, unless there are influences in his personal birthchart that are stronger than that of his Capricorn sun sign.

Appearance

The typical Capricorn man
- is stockily built

- has sharp, penetrating eyes
- rarely smiles
- has very strong white teeth
- is conscious of his appearance
- dislikes removing his clothes in public – for example, he will still be wearing a shirt during a heatwave when other men are bare-chested

Behaviour and personality traits

The typical Capricorn man

- is dignified in his manner and very polite, regardless of his origins
- seems unapproachable and self-protective
- is totally reliable in pursuit of an aim
- takes his time sizing up other people before he will relax enough to share his inner warmth
- seeks honours but is not interested in becoming famous; on the contrary, he avoids publicity
- has strong opinions but is not at all vain

 THE CAPRICORN FEMALE

If a woman behaves in a way that is distinctive of the personality associated with the zodiac sign of Capricorn, she will have a tendency towards the characteristics listed below, providing there are no influences in her personal birthchart that are stronger than that of her Capricorn sun sign.

Appearance

The typical Capricorn woman

- small and well-shaped body with slender neck
- deep, serious eyes
- has an 'earthy' beauty

- full mouth and very white teeth
- shapely legs, slim ankles, small feet

Behaviour and personality traits

The typical Capricorn woman

- is very self-conscious
- behaves in a ladylike manner in public
- dresses according to what she intends to achieve that day
- needs to gain recognition for her work
- appears as steady as a rock, but is quite moody inside herself
- runs a well-kept home, although she finds domesticity tedious
- is totally loyal to close family and distant relatives
- cannot bear to be teased
- smiles little, but when she does it is a very beautiful smile

YOUNG CAPRICORN

If a child behaves in a way that is distinctive of the personality associated with the zodiac sign of Capricorn, he or she will have a tendency towards the characteristics listed below.

Behaviour and personality traits

The typical Capricorn child

- tends to prefer older company
- often looks very old when still a baby
- is self-contained and strong-willed
- is usually even-tempered
- gets what he or she wants by slowly wearing down parental resistance

- likes the security of routine and orderliness
- has just one or two close friends
- enjoys pretending to be grown up
- usually loves reading
- likes to make things that have a practical use

Bringing up young Capricorn

Young Capricorns are not particularly enthusiastic about sport or the outdoors, so they need to be encouraged to spend time outside in the fresh air, getting some exercise. Trips out to museums, archaeological sites or even rock-climbing are likely to satisfy them.

Usually, Capricorns work doggedly at school subjects and aim to gain honours and collect certificates. It may be that they need to be encouraged to relax and play. They may seem very serious children, but they have a sense of humour; this needs to be encouraged – but not by teasing.

Young Capricorn's needs A secure, warm home with a regular routine and reliable, appreciative parents are essential to Capricorns. In spite of all their capable maturity, young Capricorns can lose self-confidence very easily.

What to teach young Capricorn Young Capricorn must be taught how to relax and take a rest from his or her responsibilities from time to time, or their life will become joyless. Young Capricorns need plenty of reassurance because they are natural worriers. Their diet and exercise routine should also be carefully handled, as young Capricorns are prone to illnesses. Their resistance to disease improves with age.

Sensitivity to other people's feelings, and an understanding of other people's difficulties, should be taught in practical situations – but without emotional pressure. Young Capricorns also need to be taught how to express their own very sensitive inner emotions, in ways that will not cause them embarrassment.

CAPRICORN AT HOME

If a person has the personality that is typical of those born with a Capricorn sun sign, home is a place for enjoying the family as much as possible, and he or she will have a tendency towards the characteristics listed below.

Typical behaviour and abilities

When at home, a Capricorn man or woman

- really enjoys providing for the family and having visits from relatives
- likes having a routine and an organized household
- wants good quality furniture and fittings
- is basically loyal to home and family
- needs home as a safe haven for personal pleasure and business entertaining

Capricorn as parent

The typical Capricorn parent

- is strict but always fair
- takes parenthood seriously
- has an ironic sense of humour
- provides the very best for the children
- is tender and sensitive
- has difficulty relating to young children, but will find it easier as they get older

- will teach the children good manners
- provides plenty of educational stimulation

Two Capricorns in the same family

Since the need for public recognition is basic to Capricornean well-being, two Capricorns in the same family will get on quite well, provided they each have an area of endeavour in which they can succeed and achieve some adulation from others. On the whole, Capricorns are not jealous people; nor are they quarrelsome, unless someone is trying to give them orders. So Capricorn siblings or spouses should remember never to try to make the other one conform to his or her ideas of how things should be done.

CAPRICORN AT WORK

At work, the person who has a typical Capricorn personality will exhibit the following characteristics.

Typical behaviour and abilities

A typical Capricorn at work
- works hard and for long hours
- likes to have some home comforts in the workplace so he or she can change and go on to another appointment, or stay all night if necessary

Capricorn as employer

A typical Capricorn boss (male or female)
- does not neglect family life for business, and family members may visit him or her at work
- is kind but expects obedience to the rules
- has a strong sense of duty and works very hard
- is not a good mixer, but others trust him or her

- does not give perks but responds when people are in need
- takes responsibilities very seriously, and so may neglect personal needs
- dresses conservatively and is well organized
- can keep complex operations moving smoothly

Capricorn as employee

A typical Capricorn employee (male or female)
- arrives a little early and leaves late
- is dependable and can carry huge workloads
- minds his or her own business
- works steadily and quietly, staying with the same company a long time
- occasionally reveals a wry sense of humour
- is conscientious and aims high (for power not glory)
- will expect a salary in keeping with the work done
- has respect for superiors, elders and those more experienced
- enjoys commonsense procedures

Working environment

The workplace of a typical Capricorn man or woman
- must be comfortable, like a home from home
- must be tidy and well organized
- should have a framed photo of the family on the desk
- must not have money wasted on it unnecessarily

Typical occupations

Any occupation that requires good organization and clever management, but which does not require the Capricorn to be the front person. Capricorns prefer to work in private. They generally make good bankers, systems analysts, bookkeepers, researchers, dentists, architects, engineers, manufacturers and politicians. Many Capricorns are jewellers, funeral directors, art dealers, anthropologists, and managers of musicians and other entertainers. They are also to be found on radio and television programmes; their quiet, unflappable natures are perfect for serious work under pressure.

♡ CAPRICORN AND LOVE

To Capricorn, love is the source of all inspiration. Shy, awkward with the opposite sex and very much private people Capricorns are, nevertheless, deeply interested in love and are reputed to be the most capable and loyal of lovers.

Capricorn in love will have many of the characteristics listed below.

Behaviour when in love

The typical Capricorn

- is slow to make approaches and never flirts for fun
- only says 'I love you' when it is meant, and does not see any reason to keep repeating it
- may worry about the emotional aspect of the relationship
- must feel financially secure to enjoy love
- is caring, considerate and committed to the loved one

Expectations

The typical Capricorn expects

- to be taken seriously

- to make a long-term commitment
- faithfulness
- privacy
- to make a home and family
- to be admired by the loved one

The end of an affair

Typical Capricorns do not have casual affairs. If the relationship begins to fail, it often takes Capricorns a long time to take action, as they have a strong sense of duty to the partner and the family. In general, they dislike divorce.

However, once a Capricorn realizes he or she has made a mistake in choosing a mate, then the parting will be abrupt and final.

If a partner betrays a Capricorn, he or she will try first to organize things so that the partner can be reunited with the family, but if the betrayal continues, Capricorns can turn rather nasty.

CAPRICORN AND SEX

When a typical, mature Capricorn makes love, it is lovemaking at its very best: to Capricorn there is no separation between love and sex. Capricorns know by instinct when they have found the right partner for this immensely important ritual. For some people sex is a release, the satisfying of one of the basic needs in life, but Capricorns want to reach a state of total satisfaction, not only for themselves but also for their partners.

CAPRICORN AND PARTNER

The person who contemplates becoming the marriage or business partner of a typical Capricorn must realize that Capricorn will take over the organization of the partner's working life. Given this, the person who partners Capricorn can expect stability, security and success.

Capricorn man as partner

He will want a partner who can help him to achieve his ambitions.

He will want to organize the business, and will expect absolute loyalty and a disciplined routine. He may assume that the partner is dependent on him.

Capricorn woman as partner

She seeks a partner who has a good, secure position in life already. She is more likely to make a bad choice of partner than the male Capricorn, but she will soon recognize her mistake. In business, Capricorn women do not often choose other women as partners.

If the partner, in marriage or business, is lost through death or similar misfortune, Capricorns of both sexes find it hard to replace the partner, and will tend to withdraw into themselves.

Opposite sign

Cancer is the complementary opposite sign to Capricorn. Both are strong-willed and may battle for supremacy concerning organization. However, Cancer can teach Capricorn how to sense other people's needs and feelings, and how to express his or her own emotions.

Opposite sign

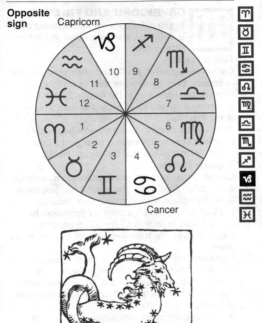

Capricorn

Cancer

CAPRICORN AND FRIENDS

In general, Capricorn likes a friend who is well bred, good mannered and not too extroverted.

Positive factors

Capricorns are loyal, kindly and often very generous to friends. They try to prove their sincerity by showing total devotion to the friendship, but this can go wrong if the choice of friend has been a bad one in the first place.

They will continue to love a friend who is old or disabled. They will not desert or neglect a loyal friend, no matter how bad the circumstances.

Negative factors

Capricorns are not very good judges of character. If a friendship goes wrong, because of bad judgement in the first place, Capricorn may turn hateful.

If a Capricorn suspects a friend of deception, he or she will start to suspect all friends. Sometimes Capricorn tests the trustworthiness of friends several times.

Capricorns have an irritating habit of organizing things that they think will be good for a friend, which the friend does not want. At their very worst, Capricorns may use a friend to further an ambition without a word of thanks.

A compatibility chart, opposite, lists those with whom Capricorn is likely to have the most satisfactory relationships.

Compatibility chart

In general, if people are typical of their zodiac sign, relationships between Capricorn and other signs (including the complementary opposite sign, Cancer) are as shown below.

	Harmonious	Difficult	Turbulent
Capricorn	●		
Aquarius	●		
Pisces	●		
Aries		●	
Taurus	●		
Gemini			●
Cancer		●	
Leo			●
Virgo	●		
Libra		●	
Scorpio	●		
Sagittarius	●		

CAPRICORNEAN LEISURE INTERESTS

Most typical Capricorns are not much interested in team sports. They will work hard at a hobby and want to make a success of it. Whatever they choose to do, it must be respectable and increase their chances of being admired or honoured.

Capricorns are so aware of their duties and responsibilities that they often find it very difficult to allow themselves to enjoy anything for its own

Capricornean likes and dislikes

Likes

- hot, simple food
- antiques, history
- duties and responsibilities
- not being pressured by others, having plenty of time
- sexual love
- privacy
- what is regarded as the best, such as a
- Rolls Royce
- membership of an exclusive club
- home and family
- colourful food
- personalized gifts
- presents wrapped in magical paper
- new books
- diamonds

Dislikes

- untidiness
- being teased
- familiarity
- surprises
- new ideas
- loneliness
- being made to feel useless
- being embarrassed in public

sake. As they get older and become grandparents, they tend to let loose a little and enjoy playing with their grandchildren.

On the whole, typical Capricorns pursue the following leisure interests:

- music, listening or playing
- golf, walking, playing chess, tactical games
- visiting museums, galleries and the theatre
- reading, gardening, improving the home

CAPRICORNEAN HEALTH

Typical Capricorns are likely to be less robust than most when they are young, but their resistance to disease increases with age. They are usually sober and temperate, so they often live to a great age.

Worry, heavy responsibilities, gloomy moods and general pessimism tend to take their toll on Capricornean health, so Capricorns need brightening up sometimes and should learn to relax.

Types of sickness

Many Capricorns seem to have some difficulty thrust upon them. Sometimes that problem may be a chronic illness but, if this is the case, they bear it with great fortitude.

Other sicknesses linked to Capricorn are rheumatism, bone diseases, sterility, damage to leg and knees, skin problems and depression.

Capricorn at rest

A typical Capricorn likes to be doing something, even when relaxing. Many are to be found doing needlework or knitting while watching television.

Parts of the body linked to Capricorn
Traditionally, the parts of the body linked with a
strong Capricorn influence are as shown in the
diagram below. Only the individual birthchart will
show if one or more of these parts of the body
have inherited a strength or a vulnerability. Any
generalization would be misleading.

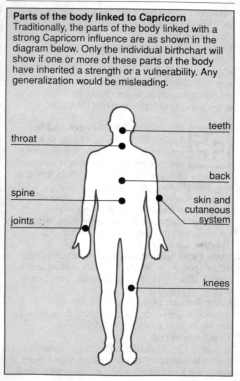

teeth

throat

back

spine

skin and
cutaneous
system

joints

knees

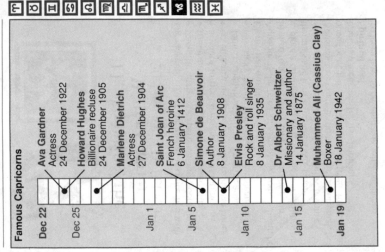

FAMOUS CAPRICORNS

Famous Capricorns

Ava Gardner
Actress
24 December 1922

Howard Hughes
Billionaire recluse
24 December 1905

Marlene Dietrich
Actress
27 December 1904

Saint Joan of Arc
French heroine
6 January 1412

Simone de Beauvoir
Author
8 January 1908

Elvis Presley
Rock and roll singer
8 January 1935

Dr Albert Schweitzer
Missionary and author
14 January 1875

Muhammed Ali (Cassius Clay)
Boxer
18 January 1942

Dec 22
Dec 25
Jan 1
Jan 5
Jan 10
Jan 15
Jan 19

11. Aquarius: the Water Carrier
20 January – 18 February

The eleventh sign of the zodiac is concerned with

- scientific analysis, experimentation, detachment
- friendship, courtesy, kindness, tranquillity
- mystery, intrigues, magic, genius, originality
- eccentricity, independence, humanitarian issues
- fame, recognition, politics, creative arts
- electricity, magnetism, telecommunications

Elemental quality

Aquarius is the fixed air sign of the zodiac. It can be likened to a paraglider, jumping off the earth to explore a rainbow, yet aware of the practicalities of thermals and how to ensure a safe landing. Air represents the mind and the ability to think; Aquarian ideas may be unusual or even original, but once formed, they tend to remain fixed. Fixed air, in brief, is a metaphor for fixed opinions.

Spiritual goal

To learn how to develop true self-confidence.

THE AQUARIAN PERSONALITY

These are the general personality traits found in people who are typical of Aquarius. An unhappy or frustrated Aquarius may display some of the not-so-attractive traits.

Characteristics

Positive	Negative
• Communicative	• Unwilling to share ideas
• Thoughtful and caring	• Tactless and rude
• Cooperative and dependable	• Perverse and eccentric individuality
• Scientific	• Self-interested
• Strong belief in humane reforms	• Unwillingness to fight for beliefs
• Independence of thought and action	• Uncertainty and lack of confidence
• Intense interest in people	• Voyeuristic curiosity about people
• Loyal friendship	
• Inventive	

Secret Aquarius

Inside anyone who has strong Aquarian influences is a person who is extremely uncertain of his or her true identity. The Aquarius ego is said to be the most precarious in the zodiac, probably because Aquarius is the sign of non-conformity. Intellectual genius, practical eccentricity and mental oddity are all linked with Aquarius.

The typical Aquarius personality has a magnetic and powerful intellect. Putting this to good, practical use is the best way for Aquarius to build an identifiable ego.

Ruling planet and its effect

Uranus and Saturn both rule the zodiac sign of Aquarius, so anyone whose birthchart has a strongly developed Aquarius influence will tend to have original, unexpected ideas. In astrology, Uranus is the planet of the unusual and the unexpected, and Saturn is the planet of applied wisdom and forward planning.

Aquarian lucky connections

Colours	violet, light yellow
Plants	olive, aspen
Perfume	galbanum
Gemstones	glass, onyx, topaz, sapphire
Metal	lead
Tarot card	the star
Animals	peacock, eagle

THE AQUARIAN LOOK

People who exhibit the physical characteristics distinctive of the sign of Aquarius often look like non-conformists.

Physical appearance

• There is a distant, dreamy look in the eyes
• Body: taller than average
• Head: in profile always noble with fine features

♈ ♉ ♊ ♋ ♌ ♍ ♎ ♏ ♐ ♑ ♒ ♓

- Neck: bends to allow head to droop forward or tip to one side when thinking
- Movement is not graceful but has purpose

THE AQUARIUS MALE

If a man behaves in a way typical of the personality associated with the zodiac sign of Aquarius, he will have a tendency towards the characteristics listed below, unless there are influences in his personal birthchart that are stronger than that of his Aquarius sun sign.

Appearance

The typical Aquarius man

- is usually taller than average
- has long bones
- may have broad hips
- is strongly built
- has a distinctive facial profile
- has a high, broad forehead

Behaviour and personality traits

The typical Aquarius man

- is unwilling to reveal his feelings
- is friendly towards everyone
- is a group person
- is fair-minded and has his own very strong, but personal, moral code
- has wide interests
- is attracted to the mysterious and the secret
- is an intuitive thinker with a very practical streak
- does not usually aim to become rich but to develop his ideas and communicate them

THE AQUARIUS FEMALE

If a woman behaves in a way that is distinctive of the personality associated with the zodiac sign of Aquarius, she will have a tendency towards the characteristics listed below, providing there are no influences in her personal birthchart that are stronger than that of her Aquarius sun sign.

Appearance

The typical Aquarius woman

- may have broad shoulders
- has a large bone structure
- has a long neck
- ignores feminine conventions, but always dresses in such a way that she looks stunning

Behaviour and personality traits

The typical Aquarius woman

- has a wide circle of friends from all walks of life
- is concerned about and deeply involved in the community
- is adept at getting people to settle feuds
- can be totally unpredictable
- has a wide variety of interests and a mind of her own
- will have a basic lack of self-confidence
- can be easy-going and accepts the many differences among people

YOUNG AQUARIUS

If a child behaves in a way that is distinctive of the personality associated with the zodiac sign of Aquarius, he or

♈ ♉ ♊ ♋ ♌ ♍ ♎ ♏ ♐ ♑ ♒ ♓

she will have a tendency towards the characteristics listed below.

Behaviour and personality traits

The typical Aquarius child

- is a quick thinker
- is sensitive and intuitive
- is outwardly calm, relaxed and delightful
- is unpredictable and full of amazing ideas
- wants to analyse everything and everyone
- does not like emotional demands
- rebels against commands and rules but comes to sensible conclusions when allowed to think things through for him- or herself
- is generous to friends
- has a huge number of friends of all kinds
- tends to be absent-minded

Bringing up young Aquarius

Young Aquarius has an enquiring and analytical mind and is constantly on the go. He or she needs plenty of opportunity to make discoveries, try out inventions and communicate ideas to others. Young Aquarius tends to be detached and dispassionate, finding close relationships difficult.

Young Aquarius's needs A peaceful, calm and harmonious environment is essential to young Aquarius, because he or she is so sensitive to underlying tensions.

Young Aquarius often looks more confident than he or she is, so parental understanding and genuine encouragement are needed. Like any child, Aquarius needs love, especially in the form of respect, listening, appreciation and friendship.

What to teach young Aquarius Their minds are always working at lightning speed, so often they get into a mental muddle. Consequently, young Aquarius should be taught how to think logically. In practical terms, they will need to be taught simple methods for remembering things and for finding their way when they get physically lost.

AQUARIUS AT HOME

If a person has the personality that is typical of those born with an Aquarius sun sign, home is a place where he or she can fully express unconventional ideas.

There are two types of Aquarius: the suave and the messy. He or she will have a tendency towards one of the sets of characteristics listed below.

Typical behaviour and abilities

When at home, a suave Aquarius man or woman

● lives in a spacious, elegant apartment filled with interesting items

● eats unusual menus of gourmet food

● enjoys having houseguests from all walks of life

When at home, a messy Aquarian man or woman:

● lives in a tiny, untidy flat filled with oddities

● eats strange mixtures of plain food

● enjoys a wide variety of friends dropping in who feel at home in a creative mess

● leaves inventions lying around

● only washes up when in the right frame of mind

Aquarius as parent

The typical Aquarius parent

● is a friend for life

- encourages independence of thought
- does not concentrate on discipline
- is prepared to discuss even adult problems
- is kind, relaxed and makes rational judgements
- does not like or encourage emotional arguments
- will want the best of modern education for the children

Two Aquarians in the same family

When married, they usually enjoy a peaceful, friendly relationship. Aquarian parents and children can also get on well, although serious personal problems may be ignored in favour of taking a broad view of humanitarian ideas. Aquarians can be quite crazy together on occasions, as they all have bright minds and are intuitive.

AQUARIUS AT WORK

At work, the person who has a typical Aquarian personality will exhibit the following characteristics.

Behaviour and abilities

A typical Aquarius at work

- enjoys working with a group
- usually likes to use his or her mind
- dislikes routine and decision-making
- enjoys variety

Aquarius as employer

A typical Aquarius boss (male or female)

- is fair and will pay employees exactly what the job deserves
- will be generous to anyone doing extra-special work beyond the terms of a contract

- although not a natural executive, he or she will carry out the role of boss using all the Aquarian skills of quick thinking and shrewd analysis
- will expect a day's work for a day's pay
- dislikes any form of dishonesty
- is unshockable
- will not forgive lies or broken promises
- will give employees all the rope they need (even to hang themselves)

Aquarius as employee

A typical Aquarius employee (male or female)

- is aloof but gathers a large circle of friends
- will regularly go off into a mental exploration of future possibilities – and return with some very creative ideas
- brings a fresh approach to any task
- will frequently change his or her job or type of occupation in the early years; later he or she will settle down and stay with one company
- is conscientious, courteous and has a knack for sensing what's wrong with machinery

Working environment

The workplace of a typical Aquarius man or woman

- could be almost anywhere in the world
- will have the latest communication technology
- changes frequently
- should be free from emotional tensions and noise

Typical occupations

Anything that involves experimentation, ideas, investigation, analysis and forward thinking attracts Aquarius. For example: dancer, scientist, photographer, astrologer, singer, TV or radio presenter, writer, charity worker, inventor, archaeologist, radiographer, electronics engineer, humanitarian aid worker.

AQUARIUS AND LOVE

To Aquarius, love is an attitude of caring for all humanity. Aquarius in love will have many of the characteristics listed below.

Behaviour when in love

The typical Aquarius

● attracts the opposite sex in the first place by their friendly open manner

● may try to seem glamorously aloof

● is afraid of a deeply emotional involvement

● genuinely wants friendship with the loved one

● will guard his or her independence jealously

● enjoys a living-apart relationship

Expectations

The typical Aquarius expects

● his wife to stay at home

● her husband to share or take over the running of the home

● personal freedom of movement and action

● loyalty and faithfulness, which Aquarius will give in full once happily married

● understanding and tolerance of his or her oddities

● the partner to enjoy frequent visits from a wide variety of friends from every walk of life

The end of an affair

The typical Aquarius has only one love affair at a time and is devoted to that partner until curiosity leads them elsewhere.

Aquarius, male or female, likes to dominate the relationship (as a way of controlling the feared emotions). A partner who makes too many demands, becomes jealous or tries to put limitations on Aquarius's freedom is usually dropped quite suddenly and may be treated like a total stranger. If the partner does not take the hint, Aquarius is quite capable of doing something to make the partner end the affair. Once Aquarius has settled into a marriage, he or she does not like divorce and will often want to remain friends with a past partner.

AQUARIUS AND SEX

When a typical Aquarius makes love it is more an intellectual experience than an emotional one. He or she will be most assiduous about hygiene and contraception. Aquarius is likely to do a lot of self-searching, but may not find it easy to listen to the partner's emotional problems.

Aquarian partners often have verbal quarrels which seem to take the place of physical contact. Affairs do not seem to bother Aquarians, and they are rarely jealous. Many Aquarians make much better friends than lovers. Sometimes Aquarius can be rather modest about sex – even prudish.

♈ ♉ ♊ ♋ ♌ ♍ ♎ ♏ ♐ ♑ ♒ ♓

AQUARIUS AND PARTNER

The person who contemplates becoming the marriage or business partner of a typical Aquarius must realize that Aquarius will need to have unlimited freedom.

Aquarius will also want to dominate the partnership in order to ensure his or her interests in the wider world are not restricted.

Given this, the person who partners Aquarius can expect loyalty, a fair share of the work and never to have the business taken away from them.

Although Aquarius has no great driving ambition, the typical Aquarius has a very fine mind (one of the best in the zodiac) and can be an asset to any venture. If fame comes their way, the Aquarius partner will happily lap it up.

Aquarius man as partner

He will want a partner who recognizes the ideas and inventiveness that he can bring to the business, and who will allow him the freedom to introduce new concepts.

Business partners contemplating asking an Aquarius to join them should first ensure that he has enough knowledge about the business.

Aquarius man wants a marriage partner who will run the home and children and be a loyal, lifelong friend. He wants a woman who is capable of looking after herself, and who will not need to lean on him.

A woman who wants a good income from a steady breadwinner should look elsewhere.

Aquarius woman as partner

So long as she is left to circulate freely among her many friends and pursue her dozens of outside interests, Aquarius woman will be a faithful partner. Although she can be tender and caring, she inhabits a world of ideas. She needs a partner who recognizes her brilliant mind.

In business or marriage, Aquarius woman will be concerned that her partner is recognized for his intellectual achievements; she is far less interested in making money. She will enjoy physical closeness, but will also be happy with long periods when the relationship remains relatively platonic.

Opposite sign

Leo is the complementary opposite sign to Aquarius. Although relations between them can be difficult, Leo can show Aquarius how to make choices to please the self, rather than for an ideal. In this way, Aquarius can build emotional self-confidence.

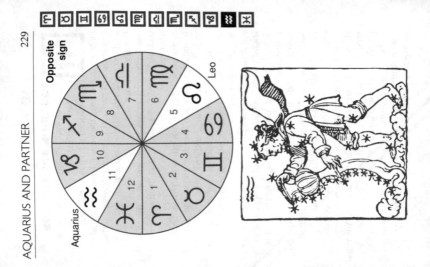

AQUARIUS AND PARTNER

Opposite sign

Leo

Aquarius

AQUARIUS AND FRIENDS

Aquarius makes many friends but has very few confidants. In general, Aquarius likes a friend who has intellectual interests and enjoys the unusual and the radical. Aquarius will be friendly towards anyone, and will tend to regard any relationship as platonic.

Positive factors

Aquarius rarely passes judgement upon the ethical codes of friends – but will expect them to live by their codes.

Aquarius will put a lot of effort into his or her friendships and make friends with anyone: rich and poor, black and white, good and bad.

An Aquarian friend is a constant source of mental stimulation, information and practical help.

Negative factors

An Aquarius will take a great interest in his or her friend's ideas, and may eventually adopt some of them as his or her own, using them whenever it is convenient.

Aquarius tends to take over a friendship, slowly but surely, and put the friend under an obligation. Aquarius also pours out troubles to friends, expecting their concerns to be regarded as more important than anything else. However, when friends need help with their own problems, Aquarius tends to draw back and tell them to ignore the problem and it will go away.

A compatibility chart, opposite, lists those with whom Aquarius is likely to have the most satisfactory relationships.

Compatibility chart

In general, if people are typical of their zodiac sign, relationships between Aquarius and other signs (including the complementary opposite sign, Leo) are as shown below.

	Harmonious	Difficult	Turbulent
Aquarius	●		
Pisces	●		
Aries	●		
Taurus		●	
Gemini	●		
Cancer			●
Leo		●	
Virgo			●
Libra	●		
Scorpio		●	
Sagittarius	●		
Capricorn	●		

AQUARIAN LEISURE INTERESTS

On the whole, a typical Aquarius will pursue the following leisure interests:

- radical arts and theatre
- music, rhythm, dance, controlled exercise
- clowning, juggling, witty comedy
- flying, parachuting, gliding
- writing his or her autobiography or a personal diary

Aquarian likes and dislikes

Likes

- fame or recognition
- thinking about self
- privacy
- rainbows, dreams, magic
- change, eccentricity, surprises
- credit cards
- telling others what needs to be done – then watching them get on with it
- weird friends
- living within their means

Dislikes

- emotion and intimacy
- people who show off
- being taken for granted
- being pinned down in any way
- any kind of hard sell
- violence and fighting
- making loans or borrowing
- conventional authority
- revealing own motives
- extravagance

♈ ♉ ♊ ♋ ♌ ♍ ♎ ♏ ♐ ♑ ♒ ♓

- scientific or creative hobbies
- local politics

AQUARIAN HEALTH

A typical Aquarius needs lots of fresh air, plenty of sleep and regular exercise to stay healthy – alas, they often do not give themselves enough of any of the three.

Young Aquarius is usually very healthy, except for the odd complaint which seems undiagnosable and goes away of its own accord.

When mature, Aquarius may suffer from nervous complaints due to their intense mental activity. They may also acquire a series of phobias. Aquarians may respond to hypnosis.

Types of sickness

They have a tendency to suffer according to the weather – which is always too hot, too cold, too humid or too dry for their comfort. Circulatory problems are linked with Aquarius.

Diseases of the blood and nervous system are common, as are varicose veins and accidents to the calves and ankles.

Aquarius is linked with the extraordinary in every way, and that includes sicknesses. Sudden, inexplicable illness can overtake Aquarius, and may then clear up equally mysteriously.

Aquarius at rest

Any opportunity to lie in a hammock in the garden and dream the day away is wonderful for Aquarius's well-being.

Parts of the body linked to Aquarius

Traditionally, the parts of the body linked with a strong Aquarius influence are as shown in the diagram below. Only the individual birthchart will show if one or more of these parts of the body have inherited a strength or a vulnerability. Any generalization would be misleading.

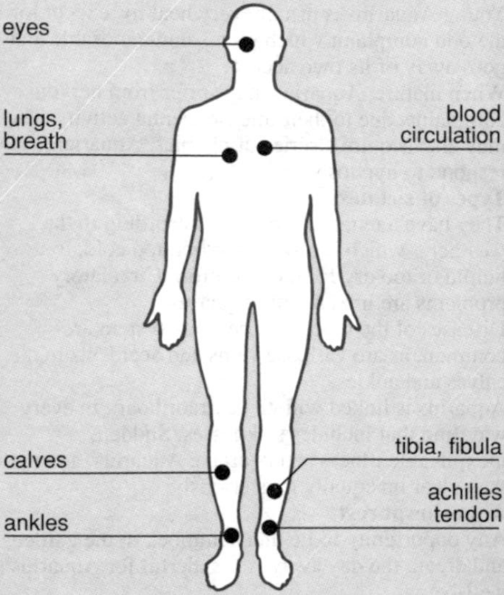

eyes

lungs, breath

calves

ankles

blood circulation

tibia, fibula

achilles tendon

FAMOUS AQUARIANS

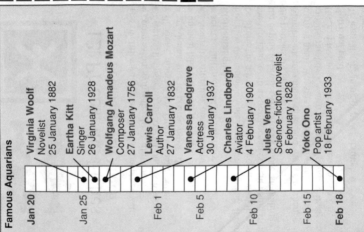

Famous Aquarians

Virginia Woolf
Novelist
25 January 1882

Eartha Kitt
Singer
26 January 1928

Wolfgang Amadeus Mozart
Composer
27 January 1756

Lewis Carroll
Author
27 January 1832

Vanessa Redgrave
Actress
30 January 1937

Charles Lindbergh
Aviator
4 February 1902

Jules Verne
Science-fiction novelist
8 February 1828

Yoko Ono
Pop artist
18 February 1933

Jan 20 Jan 25 Feb 1 Feb 5 Feb 10 Feb 15 Feb 18

12. Pisces: the Fishes
19 February – 20 March

The twelfth sign of the zodiac is concerned with

- compassion, sympathy, love, altruism
- dreams, the psychic, precognition, sixth sense
- illusions, magic, film, fantasy, make-believe
- art, drama, music, poetry, prose, dance
- unusual talent, memory, wisdom, versatility
- sensitivity, intuition, humour, satire
- secrets, fulfilment of life, eternity

Elemental quality

Pisces is the mutable water sign of the zodiac. It can be likened to a warm, turquoise lagoon, twinkling in the sunshine, or to a strong ocean current rising from the depths to break over a rocky shore, smoothing the pebbles for all time.

Mutable means changeable, and water can change its form in many ways: rain, hail, snow, mist, frost, clouds, rainbows, warm pools and puddles; thus Piscean feelings can change a dozen times a day.

Spiritual goal

To learn the meaning of peace through service to others.

THE PISCEAN PERSONALITY
These are the general personality traits found in people who are typical of Pisces. An unhappy or frustrated Pisces may display some of the not-so-attractive traits.

Characteristics	
Positive	Negative
• Loving and caring	• Self-pitying
• Trusting, hospitable and will help all in distress	• Gullible and will give all in a lost cause
• Shy	• Temperamental
• Helpful	• Dependent
• Romantic	• Escapist
• Creative	• Sensationalist
• Mystical	• Depressive
• Gentle and kind	• Can lose touch with reality
• Compassionate	• Too emotionally involved with the problems of others
• Understanding of others	• Tends to blame self for everything

Secret Pisces

Anyone who has strong Piscean influences is a person who has perhaps the most extreme choices of any zodiac sign. Pisces can accept the challenges of life and rise to the top, or can give in to the easy way of oblivion and sink to the bottom. This choice is symbolized by the two fishes.

To help him or her swim to the top, the Pisces must find peace through beauty, music and harmony.

The Pisces needs work which will enable him or her to achieve this. More than any other sign, Pisces has many talents which may be used to develop their character. Many work hard to improve the lot of humanity. Others bring their talents to film and entertainment, enlivening the lives of thousands.

Pisces needs to turn his/her private, mystical dream world of love and compassion into a reality. The only other option for Pisces is a life of illusion and, ultimately, a sense of failure.

Ruling planet and its effect

Jupiter and Neptune rule the zodiac sign of Pisces, so anyone whose birthchart has a strong Piscean influence will tend to bring benefit to others through their sensitivity.

In astrology, Jupiter is the planet of expansion, optimism and generosity. Neptune is the planet of dreams, sensitivity, the unconscious and the world of unreality.

Piscean lucky connections	
Colours	violet, light green, blue
Plants	opium poppy, lotus, water plants
Perfume	ambergris
Gemstones	pearl, amethyst, beryl, aquamarine
Metal	tin
Tarot card	the Moon
Animals	fish, dolphin

THE PISCEAN LOOK

People who exhibit physical characteristics of Pisces look more clumsy than they actually are.

They give off a feeling of other-worldliness, and usually have very sensitive, caring eyes. They may have a trusting, eager look or a quality of empathy and non-judgment exclusive to those who truly understand human sorrows and failings.

Physical appearance
- Body: usually short and thick-set
- Back: may stoop as the person walks
- Eyes: a sleepy appearance with large eyebrows
- Head: oddly shaped
- Limbs: generally short

THE PISCES MALE

If a man behaves in a way typical of the personality associated with the zodiac sign of Pisces, he will have a tendency towards the characteristics listed below, unless there are influences in his personal birthchart that are stronger than that of his Pisces sun sign.

Appearance
The typical Pisces man
- may be tall but is not physically distinctive
- has a somewhat clumsy appearance
- has rather heavy jowls
- has broad or thick shoulders

Behaviour and personality traits
The typical Piscean man
- has few prejudices

- is not ambitious for status, fame or fortune, although he can make good use of opportunities if they come his way
- is very romantic
- cannot easily be fooled
- has few material needs, but needs his dreams
- talks slowly and is knowledgeable on many subjects
- is rarely jealous, but gets hurt all the same
- is emotionally involved in whatever he does, although he may never show it

THE PISCES FEMALE

If a woman behaves in a way that is distinctive of the personality associated with the zodiac sign of Pisces, she will have a tendency towards the characteristics listed below, providing there are no influences in her personal birthchart that are stronger than that of her Pisces sun sign.

Appearance

The typical Pisces woman

- is normally slim, but tends to put on weight easily in later years
- has large eyes and an oval face
- has a clear, soft skin, whatever her colour
- has an air of feminine mystery
- has a very warm, charming smile

Behaviour and personality traits

The typical Pisces woman

- does not try to dominate her partner in any way
- often appears vague and dreamy

- is subtle and, while appearing to be helpless or incapable, gets things organized and manages the finances extremely well
- protects her emotional vulnerability with humour or a sophisticated exterior
- needs to belong to someone
- has a warm, sympathetic heart

YOUNG PISCES

If a child behaves in a way that is distinctive of the personality associated with the zodiac sign of Pisces, he or she will have a tendency towards the characteristics listed below.

Behaviour and personality traits

The typical Pisces child

- has the sweetest, dimpled smiles and the most winning ways of all babies
- lives in a world of make-believe
- dislikes orderliness and routines
- has an amazing imagination
- holds secret conversations with invisible (and sometimes long-dead) people
- has a very active sixth sense
- believes in magic, fairies and Santa Claus, and may re-invent myths
- enjoys the company of adults more than that of other children
- rarely loses his or her temper, and instead just happily goes his or her own way

Bringing up young Pisces

At school, young Pisces avoids the limelight and

does not take leadership positions, so he or she should never be pushed to take such roles. However, Piscean children are the source of wonderful ideas for play and adventure in which Pisces will be happy to let other children take the lead.

Parents would be wise to gently help young Pisces to distinguish between fantasy and reality, without destroying his or her rich imagination. Because of their passive, non-aggressive natures, Piscean children may sometimes be the victims of bullies, so it would be useful to teach them strategies for dealing with such situations.

Young Pisces' needs Young Pisces needs to feel he or she belongs to someone, or several someones. Emotional connections with people are absolutely essential to Piscean happiness. He or she is less concerned about places and things, although attachments to animals are often sought as well. Consequently, a Pisces child should be helped to believe in him- or herself and prevented from becoming too clinging. Parents who cling to their Pisces child are doing him or her no good at all.

What to teach young Pisces Piscean children absorb information and ideas like sponges, and transform everything into magic. They should be taught to sort their ideas and to distinguish between what is practical and what is not.

Young Pisceans tend to be vulnerable to those who would deceive them. An understanding of human nature and some simple, clear rules will help young Pisces to avoid the dangers – while still developing their precious skills of compassion.

Some simple routines should be taught, otherwise
Pisces may become spoilt and will dominate the
home with his or her changing desires.

PISCES AT HOME

For a typical Piscean, home is the place
where he or she will need to feel loved.
Home can be a palace or a hovel, but it
must contain people towards whom he or she is
drawn emotionally and who love him or her.

Typical behaviour and abilities

When at home, a Pisces man or woman

- will often enter a fantasy world
- will feel safe to freely explore his or her
  imagination
- will probably have no fixed routine
- is likely to be untidy, although he or she may have
  a sudden urge to tidy everything to avoid
  confusion: this can happen at any time
- should keep a large, clear clock
- will need a space for personal privacy
- will make the home itself into a wonderful world
  of art, music, design, and good food and wine

Pisces as parent

The typical Pisces parent

- can happily accommodate all the fantasies of
  childhood
- will allow a child plenty of imaginative freedom
- may lack discipline
- listens with understanding
- encourages personal development
- may have to teach the children punctuality

♈
♉
♊
♋
♌
♍
♎
♏
♐
♑
♒
♓

- is warm and loving and rarely uses harsh words
- may tend to spoil the children
- will probably have a very personal and unusual set of rules to which the children must adhere

Two Pisces in the same family

Pisces in the same family should get on very well, providing they have an outlet for their vivid, unworldly imaginations. For example, Piscean siblings may build an imaginative world together; or a Piscean parent who makes fictional films will find inspiration in the ideas of his or her offspring.

PISCES AT WORK

At work, the person who has a typical Pisces personality will exhibit the following characteristics.

Typical behaviour and abilities

A typical Pisces at work

- is rarely in an executive position, nor does he or she enjoy being tied to working in a team that has a strict routine
- enjoys work that offers freedom of expression, which usually means working alone or in a self-directed position
- if working in a team, Pisces prefers an occupation that allows for frequent changes and adaptations

Pisces as employer

A typical Pisces boss (male or female)

- is more likely to be found in organizations as a director rather than as the boss
- will serve people rather than accumulate power
- uses his or her gifts to make the correct move

- is a shrewd judge of character
- is unconventional and creative
- values those who are conventional and well organized, because they are needed to back up his or her ideas
- will never refuse help to someone in need
- may act tough to hide a deep belief in the mystical

Pisces as employee

A typical Pisces employee (male or female)

- needs work where there is plenty of outlet for either human understanding or creative imagination
- will be depressed, lazy and useless if neither of these needs are satisfied
- will be very affected by surroundings
- when happy is a loyal worker
- although nobody seems to understand how he or she operates, Pisces gets the job done

Working environment

The workplace of a typical Pisces man or woman

- must feel comfortable
- will have a pleasant atmosphere
- should be a large and flexible space
- may be brightly coloured

Typical occupations

All kinds of jobs in film, theatre, TV, radio, ballet, music and art will attract Pisces, who is often a good actor. A job that allows travel will be attractive. Advertising, public relations and any job that is part of the service industry. Helping people to solve their problems, charitable and church work are also very attractive to Pisces.

PISCES AND LOVE

To Pisces, there is no difference between love, affection and romance. A Pisces needs all three. A Pisces who feels unloved is an unhappy person to whom life seems very grey. Love revitalizes Pisces.

Behaviour when in love

The typical Pisces

- is romantic
- eager to please
- adapts to the demands of the relationship
- appears to be helpless, delicate and vulnerable, but being loved enables Pisces to cope very well with a range of difficulties, problems and tragedies
- is emotionally involved, to the point of not recognizing when he or she is being deceived or treated badly

Expectations

The typical Pisces expects

- to have his or her dreams valued, and to be protected from harsh criticism
- to be cared for romantically
- to have children (Pisces love children)
- to be frequently reassured that they are loved
- all birthdays and anniversaries to be remembered

The end of an affair

Some Pisces tend to drift into another relationship almost without noticing, yet are surprised when they are accused of unfaithfulness. The self-doubt which haunts many Pisces can only be dispelled by repeated reassurance that they are lovable. Consequently, Pisces may sometimes just leave a relationship for no clear reason and with no regrets. It is not that Pisces does not love the abandoned partner anymore. On the contrary, Pisces will often show much sympathetic understanding and will try to retain a friendly relationship with the one he or she has left.

The worst possible event for a Pisces is to be rejected by the one who loved them. A partner who wants to end a relationship with a typical Pisces will find this a very difficult thing to do. Pisces will cling, convinced that if they reform in some way, everything will be all right again. The ex-partner of a Pisces may have to go to extremes to extricate him- or herself from the emotional mess that a hurt Pisces can produce.

PISCES AND SEX

When a typical Pisces makes love it is an act of romance rather than of carnal pleasure. Typical Pisces is less interested in sexual activity than in the expressions of love that come before and afterwards.

Piscean energy is more often used up in the emotional experiences of love than in the sexual act. This does not mean Pisces is not interested, indeed he or she may seek several partners, but this is for reassurance rather than personal pleasure.

Pisces can be the least prejudiced and most compassionate of all the zodiac signs. Pisces will show a deep and real love for a partner who has problems or physical abnormalities, or who has to face a tragedy or business disaster. Sex will be one

of the expressions of love given by a caring and
devoted Piscean spouse.

 PISCES AND PARTNER
The person who contemplates becoming
the marriage or business partner of a
typical Pisces must realize that Pisces
will expect to be supported – emotionally or
financially. Given this, the person who partners
Pisces can expect loyalty and sensitive
understanding.

Pisces man as partner

He will want a partner who will work for him:
someone to run the household efficiently and who
will entertain his friends and business colleagues.
In return, the married Pisces will bring great joy to a
household with his wonderful imagination. Marriage
gives male Pisces more self-assurance, so he will
become more decisive.

Potential business partners should be prepared to
undertake the practical, administrative side of the
business, leaving the Piscean partner free to exercise
their creativity and understanding.

Pisces woman as partner

She will want a marriage partner who will support
her in every respect. To many men, Pisces is the
perfectly feminine woman. She may appear to be a
helpless, fluffy person but, once married, she will
feel secure and her reserve of talents and abilities
will pour out in every direction.

In business, a Pisces woman will be best in creative positions and in public relations, but should not be expected to do the routine office jobs.

Opposite sign

Virgo is the complementary opposite sign to Pisces. While Pisces adapts him- or herself to the emotional needs of others, Virgo works hard to serve others by responding to the needs of the moment with practical solutions. From Virgo, Pisces can learn how to translate Piscean sensitivity and understanding into practical action – thus dispelling self-doubt and building confidence in his or her Piscean abilities.

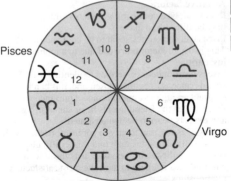

PISCES AND FRIENDS

In general, Pisces likes a friend who is useful and reassuring. In return they will give unprejudiced understanding and loyalty to their friends.

Positive factors

Pisces are emotionally attached to their friends and will rarely notice if the friend is taking advantage of this involvement.

Pisces are friendly, humorous and caring friends, even if there are long periods of time between meetings.

Pisces will always think up something interesting to do, and will enjoy any kind of artistic ventures.

Negative factors

Pisces can be a confusing person, so arrangements may be difficult to make.

Pisces can sometimes seem to be cool and off-hand. This is usually temporary and due to a moment of insecurity.

Pisces needs a hero or heroine to identify with. If a friend happens to be the chosen one, this can be pleasant enough but may become a nuisance when Pisces gives the friend talents he or she hasn't got and expects them to be demonstrated!

Pisces does not find it easy to conform; friends with conservative attitudes may find this a difficulty.

A compatibility chart, opposite, lists those with whom Pisces is likely to have the most satisfactory relationships.

Compatibility chart

In general, if people are typical of their zodiac sign, relationships between Pisces and other signs (including the complementary opposite sign, Virgo) are as shown below.

	Harmonious	Difficult	Turbulent
Pisces	●		
Aries	●		
Taurus	●		
Gemini		●	
Cancer	●		
Leo			●
Virgo		●	
Libra			●
Scorpio	●		
Sagittarius		●	
Capricorn	●		
Aquarius	●		

PISCEAN LEISURE INTERESTS

Most typical Pisces love artistic pursuits and anything that has an element of mystery, fantasy and imagination.

Pisceans love films, theatre, travelling entertainers, pantomimes, witches, monsters, elves, gypsies and mythical creatures.

Team sport is not a natural Piscean activity, but

Piscean likes and dislikes

Likes

- seafood, champagne and organic foods
- romantic places, sunsets over the sea, mountain vistas, waterfalls, ponds and waterlilies
- background music, poetry
- people who need their understanding
- mystical settings,

- candles, incense
- being loved
- freedom to drift along from time to time
- privacy
- colourful food
- personalized gifts
- presents wrapped in magical paper
- new books
- diamonds

Dislikes

- bright, noisy, crowded places
- dirty, ugly objects
- being told to get a grip on things

- stiff clothing
- authorities
- people knowing too much about him or her

Pisceans often love gentle watersports, non-competitive skiing and sky-diving.
Dangerous sports, such as racing cars, can also appeal to the Pisces because they have an unerring instinct in such situations.

PISCEAN HEALTH

Typical Pisces are healthy people so long as they feel loved and have an outlet for their dreams. Unhappy Pisces are vulnerable to problems arising from turning to drink, drugs or other ways of getting relief from what may seem unbearable emotional insecurities. Pisces often has to work hard to swim against the current that would pull him or her under. The constant effort of avoiding being sucked into oblivion is the cause of much distress to many Pisces, who, consequently, may suffer depression and other emotional problems.

Types of sickness

Troubles with the feet and toes are common among Pisces: bunions, chilblains, corns, boils and foot deformities may occur.
Pisces may become forgetful when illness is about to strike. They may also suffer from the effects of too much wine or too many drugs. The sensitive Piscean psyche suffers greatly in times of stress, and has little to draw on by way of personal resources.

Pisces at rest

A relaxed Pisces is the happiest person on earth. A chance to lie back, sip wine, listen to music and let the imagination wander is perfect bliss to Pisces.

Parts of the body linked to Pisces
Traditionally, the parts of the body linked with a strong Pisces influence are as shown in the diagram below. Only the individual birthchart will show if one or more of these parts of the body have inherited a strength or a vulnerability. Any generalization would be misleading.

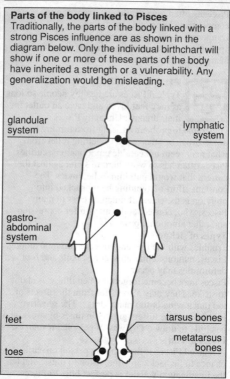

glandular
system

lymphatic
system

gastro-
abdominal
system

feet

toes

tarsus bones

metatarsus
bones

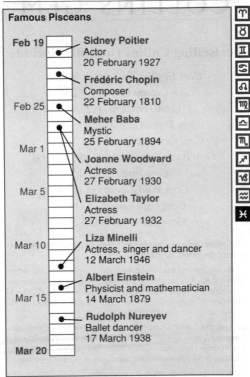

Famous Pisceans

Sidney Poitier
Actor
20 February 1927

Frédéric Chopin
Composer
22 February 1810

Meher Baba
Mystic
25 February 1894

Joanne Woodward
Actress
27 February 1930

Elizabeth Taylor
Actress
27 February 1932

Liza Minelli
Actress, singer and dancer
12 March 1946

Albert Einstein
Physicist and mathematician
14 March 1879

Rudolph Nureyev
Ballet dancer
17 March 1938